Cleopatra

Egypt's Last Pharaoh

By Laurel A. Rockefeller

Cleopatra VII: Egypt's Last Pharaoh

This book is based on events in the life of Pharaoh Cleopatra VII and constructed using primary and secondary historical sources, commentary, and research. Except when quoting primary sources, dialogue and certain events were constructed and/or reconstructed for dramatization purposes according to the best available research data. Consulted sources appear at the end of this book. Interpretation of source material is at the author's discretion and utilized within the scope of the author's imagination, including names, events, and historical details.

Check out these related Legendary Women of World History Biographies

Boudicca: Britain's Queen of the Iceni (1st Century Roman Britain)

Hypatia of Alexandria (4th to 5th century Roman Alexandria)

ISBN: 9781728670478

Laurel A. Rockefeller

EASTER EGG ALERT

Hidden inside this book are two Easter Eggs to delight fans of Doctor Who. The first Easter Egg is a character named for someone who travelled inside the TARDIS. The second is a phrase repeatedly used by the Twelfth Doctor. Using your knowledge of The Doctor (as played by David Tennant, Matt Smith, and Peter Capaldi) and series 2 through 10 of Doctor Who, go find them!

Table of Contents

Prologue

Synesius of Cyrene meandered casually through the library at the Serapeum, its massive domed roof a reminder that this was a Greek, not Egyptian, architectural masterpiece. Every few yards he stopped and looked at the shelf labels near him. Finally, after about twenty minutes he saw the small figure of his mistress standing next to a distant shelf as she organized the scrolls upon it. Smiling, Synesius approached her with a reverent bow, "Salve, August Mistress!"

Hypatia turned to him and motioned for him to rise, "What brings you to the library so early in the morning, Synesius? I thought you had reading to complete before our class this afternoon."

"I finished that reading and would like to be assigned additional texts for my enlightenment that I may understand the mind of God better," proclaimed Synesius brightly and with a touch of pride in his voice.

Amused, Hypatia tried to stifle the laugh welling up deep inside her, "A student who begs for more work! You are an unusual man, Synesius."

"I am excited and honoured to be learning from you, Mistress. You may think nothing of your fame, but your name shines as brightly as the stars themselves. Everyone has heard of you—in Cyrene, in Jerusalem, Constantinople, Rome, Alexandria, even in the cities to the north where it is said the people paint themselves blue before going into battle! Everyone knows about the great Hypatia of Alexandria; everyone wants to learn from you."

"Not the followers of this Patriarch Theophilus or the Trinitarian Christians that follow him."

"Forgive them, Mistress. They are taking their cues from Emperor Theodosius instead of thinking for themselves.

"'See to it that no one takes you captive through hollow and deceptive philosophy, which depends on human tradition and the elemental spiritual forces of this world rather than on Christ. For in Christ all the fullness of the Deity lives in bodily form, and in Christ you have been brought to fullness. He is the head over every power and authority.' Paul's letter to the Christians in Colossae. Second chapter. Verses eight through ten," quoted Hypatia. "Men like Theophilus teach that to mean what we learn here at the Serapeum is dangerous, that the books in this great library system are dangerous and must be destroyed. Even the histories of this land, the many texts about its oldest and most cherished beliefs.

"Long before this Abraham of the Hebrews was allegedly born the nisu—the kings of this land called in the Hebrew tongue 'pharaohs'— spent an unfathomable amount of money paying the most skilled craftsmen to build their tombs. Travel along the Nile and you will see them, monuments of a time long gone. Look around and you will find books that still remember what the first peoples of this land believed. Gods like falcon-headed Horus and crocodile-headed Sobek who created the Nile. Goddesses like the cow-headed Hathor and the cat-headed Bast. But of all the goddesses, none are more famous than Isis, the divine mother of kings. In ancient Egyptian her name is rendered Eset, "the seat," a reference to the throne. From Isis flows the power and the right to rule. No one may rule Egypt without her consent. Not even Rome," laughed Hypatia wistfully.

"Mistress, I am confused. Rome—or at least Constantinople—rules this land. The days of an independent Egypt are but a memory," countered Synesius respectfully.

Hypatia glided to a nearby shelf and picked up two scrolls, "Read these and understand."

Synesius looked at the titles, "These are about the Ptolemaic Dynasty?"

"Specifically, about the last of Ptolemy Soter's descendants to rule an independent Egypt. Cleopatra the Seventh, daughter of the goddess Isis, mother to Ptolemy the Fifteenth Philopator Philometor Caesar —Caesarion he is usually called. She was the last true pharaoh of Egypt and the only Greek to rule this land who spoke Egyptian," mused Hypatia. "If her life does not inspire you to see the mind of God more clearly, I do not know whose will!"

Chapter One

Antirhodos Island glittered in orange and gold with the rosy-fingered dawn as waves from the Mediterranean Sea lapped noisily into Cape Lochias. Across the cape from the island with its magnificent palace, the mighty Pharos Lighthouse kept watch over the many commercial, pleasure, and military vessels dancing, heaving, and sighing their way across to the royal harbour, to the Poseidium, and to the main port of Alexandria. Labourers emerged from their beds in their chitons and protective sandals as they welcomed what they hoped would be a profitable new day. The smell of baking bread filled the salty sea air. An ordinary day for Alexandria—or so everyone hoped.

Across the Nile Delta in the marshy port of Pelusium workers also headed to the docks to receive cargo from merchant vessels and to load empty ships with exotic goods from Arabia and from far flung routes stretching all the way along the Silk Road to Chang-An itself. Trumpets blared, forcing workers to stop what they were doing.

"Make way! Make way! Make way for his supreme majesty! King Ptolemy Theos Philopator, son of Zeus, king of kings and lord of lords!" cried the herald first in Greek and then in Egyptian as the pharaoh sitting on a cedar chair carried by eight strong slaves disembarked from the golden barge along with dozens of retainers and courtiers.

As Ptolemy processed through the port to his royal mansion, his tutor, Theodotus paced quietly near the king's throne, a report clenched in his fist. Theodotus bowed deeply as the slaves brought

Ptolemy's chair to a rest and helped him to his feet, "How was your journey, Sire?"

"I'm tired," complained Ptolemy, "tired and bored. I want some sport! Are there any criminals we can put in the arena today? I need to see blood!"

"You may get more bloodshed than you desire if these reports are accurate," previewed Theodotus.

"What do you mean?"

"Your sister, Cleopatra Thea Philopator has returned from Syria."

"If she is so stupid as to return, then we shall strike her down!" cried Ptolemy resolutely.

"If she were alone, that might be possible, Sire. I regret to inform you that she is not. Our enemies in Syria have come to her defence. They hate you almost as much as the Jews do and will do anything to see you dethroned with your body floating in the Nile for the crocodiles to dine upon. Even now her Syrian army marches on this city. In less than a fortnight we will be surrounded by land, river, and sea if we do not retreat to Alexandria," observed Theodotus.

"But I just arrived and I want blood! Her blood!" demanded Ptolemy.

"That may not be possible, Sire."

"Where is our ally—Pompey? Surely, he can help me get rid of Cleopatra! Surely he will secure my throne for me!" insisted Ptolemy.

"Defeated by Caesar at Pharsalus in Thessaly. He was last seen retreating aboard his flagship, headed for Egypt if the reports I read are accurate."

"Excellent! We will consult with him when we see him!"

Four days passed. As Cleopatra's armies closed the net around Pelusium, a Roman ship quietly pulled into the harbour. War-weary and covered in cuts and bruises earned in battle, General Pompey the Great furtively disembarked from his ship, his short grey-streaked hair covered by his palla as he slipped his way towards Ptolemy's palace.

General Achillas stopped him, "Who are you and what are you doing in this part of the palace?"

Pompey whirled around to face him, "Pompey, general of Rome and friend to the pharaoh."

"You reach us on the eve of a great siege. Are you here with an army to help us—or is it Egypt's help you seek?"

"You would not ask that question if you did not know the answer already, General Achillas. Yes, I know who you are. I would conference with Pharaoh Ptolemy this night."

"His majesty is indisposed," declared Achillas.

"What indisposes him?"

"A fit of irrational thinking. Cleopatra tightens the noose yet he would indulge in frivolities and delusions of victory. We have no victory, not while Cleopatra lives."

"Cleopatra is shrewd and well-educated—but she is only a woman!" scoffed Pompey.

"May I remind you that Ptolemy and Cleopatra's sister Bernice was also a woman—yet she wrestled power from their father, Ptolemy Auletes before she was in turn deposed and executed?"

"You Egyptians are fond of your civil wars and murders," observed Pompey.

"A habit Rome picked up from Egypt, no doubt," theorized Achillas. "And if not, perhaps Romans and Egyptians are not so different in their instincts as many in your Senate might suggest."

"I am not here to murder your young Pharaoh," asserted Pompey.

"But will you murder Cleopatra should the opportunity strike?"

"That is a conversation I must have with Ptolemy. Now, if you please, let me pass!"

Achillas met his eyes as his hidden hands gestured towards soldiers waiting in nearby shadows, "I think not!"

Suddenly twelve soldiers leapt from among the shadows, surrounding and quickly disarming Pompey. Pompey glared at Achillas, "What is this?"

"My lord pharaoh's wishes enacted. We sail for Alexandria while we still can," declared Achillas as his soldiers dragged Pompey away.

Cleopatra VII: Egypt's Last Pharaoh

Dawn broke over Pelusium. Rising early from her bed on her royal barge, Cleopatra accepted a report from the hands of one of her most trusted guards before turning and allowing her maids to dress her. Putting down the wax tablet to make her maid's job easier, Cleopatra pondered the latest report. If Pompey were now in Pelusium then Ptolemy would respond with one of two possible actions: either stay in Pelusium in hopes of turning her siege against her or flee back to Alexandria. That of course depended on Pompey's value to him as an ally. On that matter she knew Pompey was himself on the run from Julius Caesar. Logically Caesar would be in pursuit. But where would Caesar go? To Alexandria, of course! reasoned Cleopatra. Alexandria was the capital. Alexandria was the seat of power for both of them— even if the Ptolemaic hold on the city and on Egypt was tenuous at best. Thanking her maids for their assistance she pulled out fresh wax tablets and wrote instructions out for the captain of her barge in Egyptian on one and for her generals in Greek on the other before handing them off to be delivered. An hour later she felt the ship lurch forward as its sails unfurled and the ship glided back into the sea. Destination: Alexandria!

The Poseidium gleamed golden in the morning light, its massive statue of Poseidon watching over the harbour and the cape beyond. The gilded points of the god's trident glowed imposingly, a warning to all who would invade Alexandria. Silently Cleopatra's royal barge glided up to the landing steps. Covering her head and forehead with her light wool epiblema, Cleopatra found herself barely able to see as she disembarked from her ship and quietly slipped through a back entrance through secret passages to the hidden mansion within.

"Are you certain you are comfortable, my lady?" asked one of Cleopatra's ladies-in-waiting as she brought a plate of bread and fish and a pitcher of wine, the torches on the chamber walls offering the room's only light.

"I am comfortable enough. Let Ptolemy live in luxury while he can at the palace. When I am done with him he will be grateful for the gift, that fool!"

"You have a plan?"

"Always!"

"Shall I send for your generals?"

"And betray my location to Ptolemy? No! Not yet. They have their instructions. They know where I am. When this Gaius Julius Caesar arrives at the palace they will come to me! It is all arranged."

"I am glad to hear of it," answered the lady-in-waiting as she bowed to leave.

"Stop!"

The lady-in-waiting stopped.

"Have you tasted this?"

"No, my lady I have not."

"Taste it!"

"My lady I am sure it is fine!"

"Taste it!" insisted Cleopatra.

Fearfully the servant tore a small piece of the bread and put it in her mouth before taking a small bite of the fish and two sips of the wine.

"Now we wait," glared Cleopatra confidently as she sat down upon a couch. Nervously the servant paced for ten minutes before feeling a burning in her chest and collapsing in death. "Ptolemy is already returned to Alexandria. It will not be long now!"

The next morning Cleopatra slipped out of her hidden apartment and knelt at the main altar to Poseidon. Four sacred wells surrounded the fifteen-meter-tall statue that seemed tiny compared to the megalithic version overlooking the harbour. A priestess drew water from each of the wells into a single, massive chalice. Saying prayers over the chalice, she handed it to Cleopatra reverently, "May Poseidon answer your prayer, milady!"

"Thank you," answered Cleopatra in Greek. Dismissed, the priestess left her to pray. Cleopatra sipped the holy water, "Show me what to do, mighty lord of the seas! Do I come to Julius Caesar or does he come to me? Grant me your vision, your insight through this water that I may understand what escapes me. For though I am Isis reborn, I cannot see everything. —but you can, mighty lord!"

Go to the Temple of Isis, replied a voice in Cleopatra's head as she drank the holy water.

"Isis! Yes! Yes of course! The temple lies on the other side of Antirhodos Island from the palace! If there is a place to watch and wait, to hear news of both Julius Caesar and Ptolemy's movements, it would be there!"

Night fell. Under the cover of darkness Cleopatra slipped alone across the narrow channel separating the temple of Poseidon from the temple of Isis. Across smooth-paved secret paths she navigated her way to the priestess's living quarters, found an empty bed, and fell fast asleep.

The next morning Cleopatra woke to a loud clamour as Roman soldiers marched through the temple halls. The high priestess of Isis stopped them, "Why are you here? What business do you have with the Goddess Isis?"

"Pompey's body—where is the rest of it?" demanded one soldier.

"I have no idea what you are talking about," asserted the high priestess.

"This morning your Pharaoh Ptolemy the thirteenth presented my lord Julius Caesar with the head of Pompey which he hoped would please the general and secure his favour. We are here to offer Pompey a proper funeral and cremation."

"Do you Romans seek to resurrect Pompey from the dead? Is that why you come seeking Her help?"

"Resurrection? No! We are glad to see Pompey gone—but not this way! Not murdered by your Ptolemy as a gift to Julius Caesar! We seek dignity for what was once one of the greatest of our people."

"Pompey is not here—but his body is likely to either be on board my lord pharaoh's barge—or still in Pelusium if that is where he lost his head."

The soldiers bowed respectfully, "Thank you, Mistress! We will search there!"

As the soldiers disappeared from sight and sound, Cleopatra slipped into the sanctuary, "You serve me well."

"What else can I do for Isis reborn?" smiled the high priestess.

"Is it safe for me to seek Julius Caesar?"

"Not openly, Your Majesty. Though the distance is short, the palace remains well guarded by both soldiers and spies."

"Well then, it is a good thing I have magic on my side!" laughed Cleopatra quietly.

"Any news?" asked Gaius Julius Caesar as he and one of his aides marched back into the lavish apartment the general chose to be his headquarters in the palace.

"Pompey's body was found back in Pelusium," reported the aide.

"Excellent. Is his funeral done then? All of him?"

"As you have commanded so it is accomplished," affirmed the aide.

"And our efforts to locate Cleopatra?" asked the general.

"The last time she was seen was two days ago while at prayer at the Poseidium—but she has not been seen since."

"She's laying a low profile," concluded Julius Caesar. "Very wise. Clearly reports of her intelligence are not overrated."

"Well she *is* widely considered one of the most intelligent and highly educated of all the women in the world," noted the aide. "What she lacks in perfection in her flesh she more than makes up for in her wit, charm, and wisdom. I would not wish to be against her—in love or war."

"Beauty is not always about the roundness or size of a woman's breast nor in the complexion of the skin. Beauty has many forms."

"As no doubt your sexual conquests have proven," hinted the aide playfully.

"Meaning?" asked Julius Caesar sternly.

"I mean no disrespect, Sir!"

Julius Caesar waved for him to leave, "No bother! My reputation is well-earned. No one I fancy refuses my bed. No one!"

"Is that so?" asked Cleopatra as she emerged from a shadow on the edge of the room. "You are Gaius Julius Caesar, I presume?"

Julius Caesar approached her, his gait like a jaguar assessing powerful prey as he extinguished the candle on the desk in front of him, "Cleopatra the Seventh Thea Philopator, I presume?"

"You may simply call me Isis if that is simpler, General."

"How about Cleopatra? Oh, I know it is Egyptian custom to be distinguished by many bynames. Given how intermarried you Ptolemies are, it is perhaps the only way to know who is whom. Your brother is the thirteenth Ptolemy—in what? Two hundred fifty years?"

"You are well informed," noted Cleopatra as she circled the general gracefully, her own movements as elegant as those of the goddess Bast.

"How did you get in here?"

"Magic!"

"Magic? Or were you in that carpet that mysteriously appeared in this room four hours ago?"

"A goddess never reveals the secrets behind the miracles she creates."

"In that she is like every other woman," retorted Julius Caesar as he extinguished another torch from the wall.

"I heard your aide imply you know something about the subject of women."

Julius Caesar extinguished another torch, "Women and men! If I fancy someone for my bed, I am never refused!"

"Never?"

Julius Caesar met her eyes, "Not once, not ever!"

"I may prove your boast wrong."

"No! You won't!" flirted the general as he extinguished the last torch in the room and put his arm around her waist.

Chapter Two

Two days later General Gaius Julius Caesar dressed himself in the toga and full regalia of the Dictator of Rome, his white rod sceptre clinched firmly in his fist even as his mind wandered in memory. Who was this Cleopatra to affect him as no man or woman had before? In all his years he had never felt quite like this. Always it was what he wanted, he demanded of a lover that counted. He came, he saw, he conquered. That was as it should be—always. Anything less was beneath him. People were tools for his ambition, his strategies, his pleasure. Tools to be used. Tools to be discarded when they no longer suited his purposes. Even his daughter's death in childbirth barely touched his heart, as much as he grieved her and missed her. So why could he not stop thinking about every detail of Cleopatra—voice, body, and soul?

A knock sounded at the door. His aide entered. Acknowledging him, Julius Caesar glided into the throne room with the pomp and circumstance he now considered normal. Drums beat and trumpets blared. Soldiers escorted Cleopatra and Ptolemy into his presence and forced them both to their knees.

Caesar rose from his throne, "You, Ptolemy the Thirteenth Theos Philopator and you, Cleopatra the Seventh Thea Philopator are here to face judgement concerning the matter of who is to rule over Egypt. This is done in accord with the law and with the terms set down in your father's will. In this ruling I am asked to consider not only what is best for Egypt, but what is best for Rome and its citizens.

"Cleopatra: you speak Aramaic, Hebrew, Ethiopic, Greek, Latin, and Egyptian. You are well-versed in oratory, mathematics, astronomy, medicine, art, music, literature, and philosophy. You have added to the great library and guaranteed its survival by dispersing its collections across daughter libraries in the Serapeum and across Alexandria so that neither fire nor natural disaster can completely destroy it. Even here in the palace there are copies of some of the greater works, including 'On the Sizes and Distances of the Sun and Moon' by Aristarchus, the complete works of both Plato and Aristotle, and copies of works in both hieratic and demotic Egyptian whose titles I cannot begin to decipher."

Cleopatra smirked at him, "Perhaps if you spent more time reading and less time in bed with your lovers you might be able to read at least the books in demotic—it's really not that hard of a language when you think of it."

"Says the only descendent of Ptolemy the First Soter to read either form of Egyptian!" noted Caesar in Greek as he tried to conceal a grin. Regaining his composure, he met Cleopatra's eyes, "Cleopatra, as the senior ruler of Egypt, you have worked to cultivate better relations with the people of Alexandria and with Egyptians across your realm. Though you are not loved by the people you are not hated either. This I cannot say of you, Ptolemy Theos Philopator. The people hate you. You are young and clearly under the control of your advisors. You are more a puppet-king than a true monarch. You possess neither education nor wisdom. Your temperament is proven to be unstable and at times particularly petty. You lack the skills needed to rule and therefore make a poor ally to Rome, despite your attempts to please me by killing my former mentor and recent rival Pompey.

"It is therefore my decision to award full and exclusive control of Egypt to Pharaoh Cleopatra the Seventh Thea Philopator. The alliance between Egypt and Rome cultivated between your father Pharaoh Ptolemy the Twelfth Auletes is now transferred to Cleopatra and only Cleopatra. If young Ptolemy the Thirteenth wishes to contest this ruling he may do so in battle. And may the gods have mercy on his soul."

"You! You seduced him!" accused Ptolemy viciously. "You went in secret to Julius Caesar's bed and used your charms and your magic to make him decide in your favour! Sex! That is what this is about! You offered him your body in exchange for the throne! You are a whore! A whore I tell you!"

Cleopatra met her brother's eyes coolly, "Gaius Julius Caesar, Dictator of Rome has made his judgement, Ptolemy. If you value your life I strongly suggest you depart Alexandria and never return to Egypt."

"And if I refuse? If I contest this ruling?" challenged Ptolemy.

"Then my mercenaries are at his disposal, along with his own forces from Rome," declared Cleopatra. Shifting her gaze, she met Caesar's eyes, "Does my brother have your leave to depart?"

"Yes," commanded Caesar. "Be gone, Ptolemy."

Still furious, Ptolemy XIII stamped his feet as he left, never to return again.

Cleopatra returned her focus on Caesar, "Thank you, Gaius."

Caesar motioned for his aide to leave, "I did not do this for you, Cleopatra. I acted in the interests of Rome and only Rome. We need Egypt's wealth, wealth only you can deliver to us."

Cleopatra approached him and put her chin on his shoulder, "Was my brother right or wrong about you? Did the last two nights together influence your decision?"

Gaius caressed her sweetly, "I do not know! I would like to think this is only about business. But you do have an affect on me such as I have never felt before! I find myself dreaming of you when you are not with me, of wanting you as I have never wanted anyone else! I feel you in my mind, in my heart, in my very soul. It is as if I have waited all the years of my life to be with you! I do not claim to understand it! Why should I? In my ambition I have become a soldier. Believe it or not that was not by design. But when the dictator of Rome puts a price on your head, when you are forced to sleep in a different house every few days because you are politically inconvenient to those in power … it changes you I suppose!"

"What happened?"

"My father Gaius Julius Caesar after whom I was named died when I was sixteen. Needing money and being political ambitious I pursued a position as high priest of Jupiter and succeeded in that endeavour. I married my first wife Cornelia and accepted quite a favourable dowry from her father so I could keep her in comfort. Then Lucius Cornelius Sulla declared himself Dictator of Rome and everything changed. I was named an enemy of the state because his family and mine have long rivalled against each other. Before I knew it, Sulla had stripped me of my position and confiscated everything we had—including Cornelia's dowry. We were penniless. He then put a price on my head, forcing me to spend the next several weeks moving from house to house, imposing on friends of family. When the stand-off ended I found myself still alive, but without any prospects for supporting my family. I did the only thing I could think of: I joined the army," remembered Gaius.

"And that's how your military career started?"

"Yes! Funny, I haven't thought about that in a very long time. You do have an effect on me, Cleopatra. I do not understand it. I do not think I could begin to. But it's there. It's real and undeniable. I do not think myself capable of leaving your side, regardless the cost to me or even, dare I say to Rome! If I did not know better I would think I was falling in love with you."

"Love is a luxury for those who work for us. It has always been far too expensive for great leaders. We marry our positions and our titles. But I … I would be lying if I said that even my heart feels something very different when I am with you, Gaius."

Gaius kissed her sweetly, "Do I dare dream that love can be mine? Do I dare delude myself into thinking I can afford it?"

"Do I?" asked Cleopatra as she lost herself in his eyes.

"I don't know," whimpered Gaius.

"Take me to bed, here! Now! Let me forget about love! Drown me in the intoxication of pleasure, Gaius! I beg you!"

"As you command!" affirmed Gaius as he unfastened the broaches holding her peplos together at the shoulder. As the fabric fell Cleopatra opened herself to her lover's touch, sweeping aside, for the moment, all thoughts of love.

"Kaliméra," smiled Cleopatra as she woke happily in Gaius' bed, the night's passion whirling about in her memory. Opening her eyes, she noticed Gaius already dressed, his aide helping him put on his armour. "Gaius? What's going on?"

Gaius crossed the room and kissed her sweetly, "I'm sorry, Cleopatra. I woke you."

"You should have woken me earlier. What is happening?"

"I can no longer defer to my commanders. I must join our forces and lead them myself. Your brother is choosing to fight. What was once simply a skirmish in Pelusium and a siege of the city is now an all-out civil war. As much as I want to stay in the palace, I am afraid that would be unwise. Plus, the only way I can guarantee your safety is to lead them myself."

"Let me come with you to the front lines!"

"Cleopatra, darling! You know I cannot allow that."

"I am leader of men too! I have led men into battle. I can help!" pleaded Cleopatra.

"My forces are mostly Roman and what I have are loyal to me and me alone. A personal loyalty. They serve me. They won't serve you!" insisted Gaius.

"How many troops do you have?"

"Not enough, but a small scout ship departs for Rome on the next tide with my requests for reinforcements, along with my reports to the senate of course. Without those additional men, I cannot defeat your brother, even with my tactical genius."

"You've been outnumbered before! Many times! Only four years ago you defeated the full might of Gaul under the command of their leader Vercingetorix at the Battle of Alesia. Why should this be any different?"

"It won't be—once reinforcements arrive. In this you must trust my judgement! Please, darling! Trust me! I know what I am doing."

Cleopatra rose and pulled a tunic dress over herself, "I do trust you." Sweetly she embraced him from behind, "But I do not want you to go."

Gaius turned around and kissed her, "I do not want to go either, not like this! Not with you on the verge of tears. I wish you would have stayed asleep so I could have slipped away quietly in the warm glow of your skin in the first light of rosy-fingered dawn, the memory of the night fresh and glorious in my mind."

"What do we do, Gaius about these feelings these months have grown inside us?"

"Only what we can do! We are prisoners to love, to each other. And though I would rather stay here and direct my forces from the comforts that come with being with you, I find I cannot neglect my duties—not any longer. I am Dictator of Rome. I must remain the man I was. Love must not unman me and make me its slave."

"I would not unman you with my love, Gaius! I would not wish you be anything other than who you are!"

Gaius kissed her, "I know! Now, darling I must leave you for a while. But I promise I will return to you—alive. I will find victory. You will be safe—both you and your throne. I swear it!"

Three weeks later, the promised re-enforcements arrived. At the Battle of the Nile General Gaius Julius Caesar engaged Ptolemy XIII's forces and defeated them. Fearing capture and humiliation, Ptolemy fled the battlefield. Moments later his drowned body was seen floating briefly before disappearing from the surface, never to be seen again.

Chapter Three

Cleopatra's throne room in the palace glittered with pomp, circumstance, and with the wealth of both upper and lower Egypt on full display. Onyx floor tiles gleamed like obsidian against richly carved precious wood panels on the walls. More than any other place designed for the living, this is where the wealth and power of Egypt manifested itself in the hearts and minds of the Mediterranean world.

Musicians from the known world played triumphantly on their instruments. Lyres and auloi, drums of every size and shape, trumpets, horns, harps, and pipes all filled the air with exotic music. Dancers danced acrobatically. It was a grand display designed to awe all who witnessed it.

At the end of this grand procession came the heavily pregnant Cleopatra with Gaius Julius Caesar walking three paces behind her triumphantly as if her coronation were his own. As the rituals continued in Greek, Latin, and Egyptian, Caesar could not help but to beam with pride—not only for his success in providing Cleopatra with her throne in her own right (albeit with her younger brother Ptolemy XIV officially her husband and co-ruler) but for the growing child now showing across her belly. Solemnly and at the proper moment in the rituals Caesar placed the double crown of upper and lower Egypt upon Cleopatra's head as she received the crook and fail from a high priestess.

That night Gaius and Cleopatra celebrated her coronation in bed, the ever-experienced general navigating around her pregnancy with the skill of a notorious serial adulterer. It would be the last time before her great labour pains began.

Three months later, Cleopatra screamed in pain as the baby planted in her by Caesar decided it was time to be born. Heaving and sweating profusely, Cleopatra felt as if she were given birth to an entire planet and not one human boy. Finally, after several hours of intense pain, her efforts were rewarded. As the midwife put the baby into her arms, Cleopatra looked into his deep brown eyes. Here was a boy who looked just like his father. Here was a Caesar.

One-month later Cleopatra glided herself into the healing waters of the Nile, her body still not feeling completely normal and healthy after giving birth. Things felt odd inside her when she moved or when she took a bowel movement. Pregnancy and childbirth had changed her physically in ways no one at court was about to explain to her. Quietly she said a prayer, "Horus? Can you hear me? Please, mighty one! Heal my body! Let me be whole again. Let the child I have given my Gaius grow strong in love and in your wisdom and the wisdom of Isis! Let me grow strong too. I feel so weak. My body betrays me. Why does it betray me when I have conquered the dangerous business of childbirth? I should feel omnipotent now—but I don't. Please, mighty one, by the power of the Nile I ask you: make me whole again. For my country, for my Gaius, and most of all, so I may serve you!"

"I had no idea you felt that way about yourself," observed Gaius as he slowly approached her from the shore. "You are always so confident, always so much in command of everything and everyone around you—including me."

Startled, Cleopatra turned towards him, "How long have you been there? I did not invite you. I fully expected to be alone."

"You will be alone—soon enough."

"What do you mean?"

"I mean I must leave Alexandria and sail back to Rome."

"You are displeased with your son."

"No! Not at all. I couldn't be happier or prouder—though I think your brother is jealous."

"Ptolemy the Fourteenth is barely capable of fathering children. Not like I would want to anyway. You know I never let any of my brothers take me to bed. I have but one lover and one love of my life," confessed Cleopatra as Gaius swept her into his arms and kissed her tenderly.

"Me too!" smiled Gaius. "For all my conquests and all my marriages, I have truly loved only one woman in my life: YOU!"

"Then why must you go? Why not be king of Egypt? Surely that is as good as anything Rome can offer you!"

"Don't tempt me!"

"Why shouldn't I? You love me. I love you! Stay here! Stay and rule with me. Be here and raise our son with me! Don't you want to?"

"I've never wanted anything so dearly in my life, Cleopatra!"

"Then stay!"

"I will stay if you ask me to—but not forever. I have a wife and I have responsibilities I cannot ignore nor postpone indefinitely."

"Your responsibilities I can respect. Your proper Roman wife, I cannot! I hold in my hands a power that no Roman woman can ever match! Surely a man of ambition can see that! Surely that gives me a value that she cannot offer you."

"Calpurnia is a good woman. She doesn't say much and she's certainly not very political. But her father was consul and her brother appears to be ambitious as well. It is a good alliance that makes me look good in the senate."

"A consul of Rome is no equal to the pharaoh of Egypt."

"This I will grant you. And believe me, your power and authority here make you an attractive ally," affirmed Caesar.

"But?"

"But the reality is this: the Ptolemaic dynasty is weak. It holds onto power by a thread. At any time, you can be overthrown by the citizens of Alexandria alone. And if the rest of Egypt should join in a revolt? You would be finished in days!"

"They wouldn't dare! Not with you as my ally."

"Cleopatra, listen to me: no alliance stands forever. You admire me for my ambition and my skills at getting exactly what I want. But there is a dark and dangerous side to allying your kingdom with Rome. For what do you think happens when Rome wants more than an alliance and wants to rule Egypt directly, as a province controlled by the senate instead of an ally ruled by a friend as it is now?"

"Rome wouldn't dare!" cried Cleopatra in outrage.

"Tell that to the Aedui, our first ally among the Gauls. When their king unwisely chose to join Vercingetorix in his campaign against us my legions and I crushed them and enslaved their nobles. They are no different than the rest of those Gallic barbarians. The alliance did not protect them from their fate. If anything, it hastened their demise."

"Rome will not do that to Egypt! You will ensure it!" demanded Cleopatra.

"Advocate for Egypt under your rule, yes. Ensure it? Even that is beyond my power. You want to keep Egypt as a friend of Rome instead of a province of Rome? Then send me on my way back to Rome."

"And to Calpurnia's bed?"

"Yes."

"That she may not have!" asserted Cleopatra.

"That she must have if you expect to remain pharaoh."

"You would betray me by sleeping with that … commoner?"

"She's not a commoner."

"She is to me!"

Gaius took her hands gently, "Cleopatra, please be reasonable!"

"Reason says you stay in Egypt. Reason says you raise your son—not go to bed with your wife!"

"Reason says I make a good show of Roman values and Roman ideals, that I curry favour within the senate and make Egypt look more useful as an ally than a province."

"Have I no say in this then, Gaius?"

"I am sorry, my love, but no! I will stay with you a little longer if you will tolerate me, but not forever. I will return to Rome and I will do what I can to protect Egypt—by whatever methods are necessary."

Cleopatra sat at her desk writing in fluidic demotic Egyptian. A knock sounded at the door, "Come!"

Cleopatra's court physician entered her presence with a bow, "You asked to see me?"

"Yes, Lateef! Thank you for coming at so short notice."

"It sounded urgent."

"Urgent, no. But I am glad you responded so swiftly. That is of help to me."

"How may I be of service?" asked Lateef.

"As you know I've been researching everything I can find regarding Egyptian, Greek, Roman, and Syrian medicine."

"If the Romans had been less negligent when they set fire to your late brother's ships there would be no doubt more books for you to consult," sniped Lateef brazenly.

"No doubt," agreed Cleopatra. "Fortunately, we Egyptians are smarter than the average Roman and had the good sense not to place all our books in one building. The loss of one part of our great library system is grievous indeed, but hardly devastating."

"It pleases me greatly to hear you refer to yourself as 'Egyptian' instead of Greek, Your Majesty."

"I am pharaoh. Whether the people fully realize it not I am Isis reborn! I belong to the people and to the land as much as anyone buried in the Valley of the Kings."

"I am glad to hear it."

"Thank you! Now, wise Lateef, the reason for my summons: having consulted numerous books from around the world I would like you to assist me on my book. I think I have almost everything down now, but I have not worked on patients before and I would like a fresh set of eyes on it, eyes that know more about healing the sick than I do. Will you help me?"

"Egypt is enriched by your scholarship and your passion for learning," grinned Lateef. "Of course, I will help you any way that I might."

"Thank you! Now please, come here and look at this paragraph right *here*!"

Two months later the flower of the Mediterranean's intellectual elite assembled at the Serapeum, home of one of the Great Library's most extensive collections. Greeks, Romans, Egyptians, Syrians, and Alexandrian Jews all meandered through the corridors connecting the Serapeum's many classrooms as slaves and servants served them food, beer, and wine imported from across the known world. In the amphitheatre actors performed new plays along with traditional favourites from Greece. Musicians performed. Dancers danced. It was a grand celebration of arts, sciences, and learning.

At the centre of the celebrations stood Cleopatra, her face radiant as the best and brightest gathered around her to listen to her wisdom, her insights, and her poignant questions to each and every one of her guests. Debates flared. Tempers rose at times, but ever at the centre of it all stood Cleopatra's roaring intellectual prowess. Though she was not the most physically beautiful woman in the room, none could deny she was the wisest.

As the day's festivities flowed from morning to afternoon to evening, Lateef approached Cleopatra, "Your festival is a mighty success!"

"It will be a success if those attending regards 'Cosmetics' a work worthy of inclusion in the Library along with the greatest of books on medicine."

"Surely you do not need their opinion to make it available to others to read!"

"No, of course not. But I would have their endorsement and their praise. Alexandria is the intellectual centre of the world. I would not have its reputation tarnished by writing books only courtiers could praise."

"No one doubts your intelligence, your wit, or your skills as a writer, Your Majesty."

"No one doubts it because I am pharaoh. If I were a lesser woman though would they feel the same?"

Lateef took her hands gently, "Yes, Your Majesty, I think they would. It is not your status as our pharaoh that makes your research and writing worthy. You are worthy in your own right for learning like yours shines brighter than even the great lighthouse. Stand confident, Your Majesty. You elevate the ranks of scholars, compelling us all to do our best work. We are better because you are in the world."

Chapter Four

The Seven Hills of Rome glittered like a majestic jewel made of marble, the columns of its stately public buildings standing as a testament to the growing empire's engineering might. From inside the quiet villa that was her home with her philandering husband Calpurnia watched and waited for her husband to return from the senate. That is, if he had any intent on returning to their villa at all. Rumours swept across Rome: Cleopatra was coming to Rome – and bringing her son, Gaius' bastard by that Egyptian whore, to be formally recognized as such under Roman law. An heir—but not of their marriage bed or of any respectable bed.

Finally, just as the sun began to set, Gaius arrived and kissed her sweetly. Calpurnia met his eyes coldly, "Has she arrived?"

Gaius returned her icy stare, "What business is it of yours?"

"I am your wife."

"Yes, I have noticed that. Have you forgotten?"

"Respectable Roman society will not let me forget. They say you are in love with her. Is it true?"

"Does it matter to you? Really? What could possibly be materially different between Cleopatra and some other girl—or boy—that I might choose to sleep with on any given night?"

"She is Egyptian—not Roman!"

"You think my conquests are limited to just Romans? I have taken barbarians of every colour, rank, and profession to my bed –or nearly every. When I want someone for my bed, she or he comes to my bed—you included!"

"Not tonight I will not."

"I wasn't asking you to."

"Good. Because while that whore from Egypt is here I will not consent to you using me to look respectable."

"If I demand you at my side in public, you will attend me."

"Yes, I will obey. But there is a difference between walking beside you on the streets of Rome and receiving you in my bed chamber. So please, don't bother asking me again for that privilege. There are far more interesting options for you than me!" asserted Calpurnia.

Caesar motioned to a slave, "Good! I'm glad that's settled. Now, if you don't mind, I am hungry and want my dinner."

Two days later Cleopatra's royal barge glided into port. Quietly and without fanfare, the pharaoh took her son's hand and stepped onto Roman soil, entering the villa prepared for her by Caesar on the edge of town. Attended by very few, Cleopatra relaxed. Here, at long last, she could be a lover, a mother, a woman without the confines of a court to flatter and obey her and without the pressures of protocol. She was simply Cleopatra.

One week passed. Smiling and a bit sun-burned, Cleopatra glowed with joy as she returned to her villa. A knock sounded at the door which opened unceremoniously. There stood Gaius Julius Caesar, his laurel wreath awarded during the day's Triumph glistening from the misty rain that fell ever so slightly. Cleopatra kissed him, positioning his hands on her body provocatively. Quietly Gaius carried her to bed.

Two sensuous years in Rome passed. Though his duties sometimes kept him away from Cleopatra and the delights of her bed, sometimes for weeks at a time, Gaius Julius Caesar always returned to it, making Cleopatra and Caesarion priority over all other personal relationships. In public, Calpurnia pretended not to mind. This was Caesar being the man he always was—long before their politically-advantageous marriage. As the months passed, Caesar grew in power and prestige until, at long last, a group of senators realized just how far Caesar's ambition took him. This man must be stopped—whatever the cost—if the Republic were to survive.

"My lord Caesar! What a surprise!" asked Ectorius as his last client left his humble shop. "What can I do for you?"

"Salve, Ectorius!" greeted Caesar. "I come for your advice on a personal matter."

Ectorius ushered him towards a comfortable seat, "If my talents may be of service, I offer them freely. What's on your mind?"

"My wife dreams a dream, a prophesy perhaps. It comes to her often of late. I wish to know if it is only a dream or if it is a message from the gods. Can you see for me?" asked Caesar as he sat down.

"Give me your hands," commanded Ectorius. Grasping Caesar's fingers tightly, Ectorius lowered himself into a well-practiced trance. "Your wife dreams of your death. You wish to know if she is right and you are to be murdered."

"Yes," confirmed Caesar.

"I see a plot," confirmed Ectorius. "Two men stand against you, men of power and influence. Do not come when they call for you. Do not come to the senate. Stay home. Stay away from people until you depart on the eighteenth as planned."

"Must I stay away from Cleopatra as well?" asked Caesar.

"There is great danger all around you. If you leave your home there can be no guarantee you will return home alive," repeated Ectorius. "Until the eighteenth go nowhere. The plotters will and must strike soon, before you can leave."

"Thank you, my friend. I will abide your warning. I will not leave my home until I am ready to board my ship," affirmed Caesar.

But promises are hard to keep. The morning of the fifteenth of March arrived. Despite all intentions to stay home, Caesar found himself lured into the streets of Rome by Decimas whom he trusted. Decimas took Caesar into the theatre built by his former rival Pompey that was the temporary meeting place for the senate after a recent fire destroyed the senate building. There Gaius Julius Caesar met his fate as over twenty senators stabbed him to death. Hours later Calpurnia, Cleopatra, and Caesar's friend and ally Marc Antony attended his state funeral as Caesar's body was cremated among throngs of adoring Romans wishing to honour their dear leader. As Calpurnia carried out her late husband's will and dissolved his estate, Cleopatra and Ptolemy Caesar set sail for Egypt, never to return to Rome again.

Chapter Five

"News from Rome!" heralded the Roman soldier, his reddish hair and blue eyes piercing through his armour awkwardly as the heavy wood doors to Cleopatra's throne room reluctantly obeyed their masters to admit him.

"What news from Rome?" asked Cleopatra, the annoyance in her voice making it clear she did not wish to be interrupted from her engaging conversations with the three men around her.

"Gaius Julius Caesar named an heir in his last will and testament," declared the soldier.

"Who?" asked Cleopatra, her interest suddenly kindled.

"Gaius Octavius, grandson to his sister Julia. In his will Caesar adopted him and made him heir to both his political and financial fortune. Octavius has accepted the bequest despite Marc Antony's refusal to release the money needed to host the games demanded in Caesar's will as part of his new status as the heir. There is conflict now between Antony and the newly proclaimed Gaius Julius Caesar Octavianus. As a result, the senate has elevated Octavius to their ranks in defiance of Antony," reported the soldier.

"Octavian is now a senator?" scoffed Cleopatra. "He is eighteen and still a boy!"

Acknowledging her with a respectful nod, the soldier continued his report, "Perhaps, Madame, but that 'boy' as you call him is now in control of the senate's military forces. With Octavian in control, the senate's legions drove Marc Antony out of Italy and into Gaul."

"You are from Gaul, are you not?"

"Yes, Madame."

"What tribe?"

"Arverni, Madame."

"Any relation to Vercingetorix?"

"You are very well informed to know he was Arverni!"

"I make a point to know as much as I can about everything. The learned men you saw around me as you entered this chamber are scholars and leaders within the Jewish community here in Alexandria. It may seem foreign to you as a Gaul, but here in this city Greeks, Jews, and Egyptians all live in harmony together. Conflicts happen sometimes, but they are very rare I am pleased to say."

"I have not yet seen your city, Madame."

"Well then you must before you return to your duties," suggested Cleopatra with a smile as she motioned his dismissal.

"What do you expect to happen?" asked the kohen as he returned to Cleopatra's side.

"I do not know. That is not revealed to me yet. But my instincts tell me that Marc Antony will not stay in Gaul for long. From what I could tell of his character and reputation, I suspect whatever disagreements stand between him and Octavian will not soon be resolved."

"Do you think more blood will be spilled?"

"That is a given, my friend. The better question therefore is how soon will this war between them reach Alexandria and what will it cost Egypt?"

"You sent for me, Madame?" asked the minister as he entered Cleopatra's presence with a bow.

"What is the latest on Octavian and his civil war against Marc Antony?" asked Cleopatra as she sat at her desk, a series of reports scattered across it aimlessly.

"After two and a half years the war continues without a certain victor militarily," answered the minister.

"And politically?"

"Octavian is Caesar's heir. The people accept him as his heir and follow him as they would have had Caesar lived."

"As they would have had Caesar lived? The senate despised my Caesar and distrusted him. Perhaps with good cause. He was, after all, quite shrewdly ruthless."

"Perhaps in death his legacy improves in the eyes of the senate and the people?" suggested the minister. "Like a fine Italian wine."

"The people have essentially chosen Octavian then?"

"If I were a betting man, I would not put my money on Marc Antony's chances."

"What is Octavian's view on Egypt?"

"Egypt? What are we but another territory to annex? Even Babylon answers to Rome."

"Rome? Or Marc Antony?"

"Does it make a difference?"

"Yes. Yes, it does."

"What do we know of Marc Antony's character?"

"He is your typical Roman general—vain, hot-headed, and with dreams of glory. He has an eye for all things of the orient. In this he is most different from Octavian."

"You suggest Antony respects the cultures of what he and Octavian view as the 'eastern Roman empire?'"

"Octavian is a creature of Rome; Antony is inquisitive about the east. He likes our food, our history, our temples and monuments. He even respects the way we pray."

"And our women of course?"

"It would be fair that he prefers the bed of a Babylonian whore to that of a proper Roman wife."

"Antony is married, is he not? To … what is her name? Fulvia, daughter to Marcus Fulvius Bambalio of Tusculum?"

"Yes. Octavian's wife Claudia is her daughter from her first marriage to Publius Clodius Pulcher."

"Marc Antony is step-father to Octavian's wife?"

"Yes."

Cleopatra sighed, "No wonder they are at war!"

"Why did Antony marry Fulvia?"

"Money."

"Just like my Gaius! He'll do anything for money if he needs it to gain power."

"You read the situation well, Madame."

"Wars are expensive. Antony must be desperate for money after two and a half years locked in a power struggle against Octavian," reasoned Cleopatra. "I am the richest woman in the world. If he has a brain at all, he will come begging to me."

"When he does, will you give him what he asks?"

Cleopatra met the minister's eyes, "Only if he pays my price."

"What do you want?"

"A free Egypt and power enough over this region to guarantee we stay free forever! Octavian would have us as just another province. Antony—Antony might actually give us what we want," mused Cleopatra as the wheels in her sharp mind turned.

"My lord general," bowed the centurion as he approached Marc Antony from his headquarters in Tarsus.

Marc Antony met his eyes, "What is it? Any news regarding our request for Cleopatra of Egypt to meet with us here?"

"Her royal barge glides up into the Cydnus River, approaching Tarsus."

"How soon should we expect her?"

"She should reach us by mid-afternoon, my lord."

"Excellent. Has she sent a messenger?"

"No, my lord, but she has received your ambassador."

"And?"

"He reports that she will not leave her barge. Tarsus is far too dangerous for a woman of her rank and reputation. She has no desire to be kidnapped and sold into slavery."

"Given the city's reputation, I suppose that is reasonable," reasoned Antony. "Will she come if we send an escort, a bodyguard of perhaps fifty veterans?"

"No, my lord, she will not. As instructed, your ambassador offered her as much—even suggesting one hundred men if that is what would satisfy her needs for security. She declined every offer, each time with logical and astoundingly practical counter-arguments."

"Are you saying she out-negotiated Caecilius? There's not a man in Pompeii who can do as much!"

"Pharaoh Cleopatra Thea Philopator is no ordinary woman."

"No argument there," smiled Marc Antony. "What then does she want? How can I meet with her if she refuses to even consider leaving her barge?"

"Perhaps a more personal approach is required, my lord. Come to her. You lose nothing by appearing in person to meet her barge when it docks. If she approves she will send someone to invite you aboard," suggested the centurion.

"Excellent! A splendid idea! Assemble an honour guard. We will impress her from the banks of the Cydnus and earn that audience!"

That afternoon Marc Antony dressed in his finest uniform, the golden embroidery on his cloak shining brightly under the hot Turkish sun. Drummers and trumpet players heralded his arrival on the banks of the Cydnus as one hundred of his finest soldiers marched in perfect unison as they made their way along Tarsus' well-worn paved streets. Caecilius met Antony with a humble bow, "My lord general!"

"Any change since your last report, Caecilius?" asked Antony.

"No, my lord! As you can see, she is not yet arrived though if I judge distance correctly her rowers will soon close the distance and she will be here any moment now," reported Caecilius.

"Excellent."

"My lord, may I ask a question of you?"

"Of course."

"Why did you choose me to represent you?" asked Caecilius, his eyes not daring to meet the general's.

"Why shouldn't I?

"I am not a citizen. I hold no special place of honour or wealth."

"You may not hold the prestige that many in military service possess, but you are a good and honourable man, loyal and dedicated to the job at hand. I need such men," replied Marc Antony as the sound of Cleopatra's rowers at long last filled the air.

Ten minutes later, Cleopatra's barge dropped its anchors as its crew threw heavy ropes to moor it along the wharf's posts. The barge's purple sails fluttered as a wide ramp lowered into place to connect the top deck with the dock. Marc Antony and his retinue advanced upon the dock as musicians played from both the wharf and on board the barge, creating a strange but still melodic cacophony.

From behind a series of semi-sheer curtains Pharaoh Cleopatra emerged, her Grecian gown styled to resemble classical images of the goddess Aphrodite even while wearing her Egyptian collar of state in its gold and lapis beads and with a carnelian cabochon carved in the shape of a scarab over her heart protectively.

With a nod granting permission to come aboard, Caecilius strode up the steep ramp and bowed before the queen, "Thank you for coming, Your Majesty."

"Your service does you credit, Caecilius. You are most welcome here," acknowledged Cleopatra graciously.

"My master Marc Antony waits for you on the dock below."

"Yes, I can see him. His armour is not as grand as my Caesar's was."

"He wishes an audience with you. Perhaps a grand banquet at his headquarters this evening."

"My answer is still no. I will not leave my barge," asserted Cleopatra as she studied Caecilius' face.

"My lord would be greatly disappointed if you refused him. He is so eager to meet you."

"I am not refusing him audience. I am refusing to leave my barge. Tell him I will receive him at sunset and tell him to try to impress me if he seeks more from me than simply to look upon my face. If he will agree to come aboard, I promise him a supper and entertainments he is not likely to forget."

"You do not wish to receive him now to communicate your invitation?" asked Caecilius nervously.

"Correct," asserted the pharaoh. Softening she touched the ambassador's hand with a smile, "This is not to create tension between you and your master. But it is how it must be. I am pharaoh. I am to be obeyed, not treated as Gaius Julius Caesar's one-time mistress. If Antony wishes to speak to me he must do so under my terms, not his. Do you understand?"

"I do," nodded Caecilius.

"You are a good man, Caecilius. I do hope you will attend tonight as well, please."

"I am honoured! Thank you! May Isis and Athena both smile on you tonight."

"Until then, noble Caecilius," dismissed Cleopatra.

Cleopatra VII: Egypt's Last Pharaoh

Sunset glowed over the Cydnus River, the light transforming its deep blue water with shades of orange and mauve. Upstream the river's waterfall crashed and gurgled with excitement to the delight of families picnicking along its banks. On board Cleopatra's barge music played optimistically as Marc Antony, dressed as the god Dionysus strode confidently up the ramp to the top deck, the loyal Caecilius two paces behind him respectfully.

Cleopatra met them as Caecilius bowed before her, "Your Majesty, may I present to you Marcus Antonius, general of Rome. My lord, may I present to you Cleopatra Thea Philopator, Pharaoh of Egypt."

"Salve, Marcus Antonius!" acknowledged Cleopatra.

"Ave Cleopatrae!" saluted Marc Antony with a respectful bow.

Cleopatra motioned for him to rise and walk with her, "Come! Now you are aboard we can set sail."

"Where are we going?"

"To a less industrial part of the city. You Romans call the river the 'Cydnus' but locally it shares the same name as the city: Tarsus."

"You just arrived. How do you know that?"

"I make a point to know a great many things, General. Or do you think learning is the exclusive domain of men?"

"I would not dare make such a supposition, not in your divine presence at any rate," grinned Antony, his confidence wavering slightly in his voice.

"Tonight, I am Aphrodite whom my ancestors honoured centuries before Alexander the Great founded his city. Yet in my heart I am Egyptian, even if my pedigree says otherwise."

"You look every bit the goddess of love," flattered Antony as he and Cleopatra processed into the banquet room one deck below.

46

"And you style yourself as Dionysus, god of wine."

"I hope I appear as a god to you," offered Antony.

"We shall see!" teased Cleopatra warmly as she and Antony sat down at the head table, Caecilius placed on the other side of her in a place of honour and respect.

Wine flowed. The smell of Turkish spices filled the air as servants brought out a dizzying array of exotic cuisines representing the entire known world for them to sample. With each dish, Cleopatra offered its name in its native language along with a story or two about the food or the culture it came from. More than the wine, which Antony could drink deeply without obvious drunkenness, Antony felt dizzy from Cleopatra's obvious display of her superior intellect and learning. As the food and entertainment flowed around him, Marc Antony found himself dumbstruck by the sheer grandeur of the costly spectacle. If this was a tiny taste of the wealth Egypt possessed, then surely Cleopatra possessed the resources he needed to first defeat the Parthians and then Octavian.

Caecilius for his part watched with pleasure as his master sat daunted by the pharaoh's parade of food, entertainment, and knowledge. Humility was perhaps a bitter pill for a proud Roman like Marc Antony to take, but for him as a common man of humble birth it seemed fitting to him. The great Marcus Antonius, de facto joint ruler of the empire with Gaius Julius Caesar Octavianus was as proud as his rival, often at the expense of freeman, women, slaves, and non-Romans. One night of Cleopatra's obvious superiority could only do him, and the empire, good.

Marc Antony woke to find himself in his own bed at his headquarters in Tarsus. As the sun pierced into his bed chamber Antony struggled to remember how he ended up from the luxurious delights of Cleopatra's barge and back in his own bed. Dazed and confused and slightly sick from a hangover, Antony summoned a servant to help him dress and eat something. That is, if the throbbing agony in his head would ever calm down.

Two hours passed. Finally feeling better, Antony found Caecilius sitting quietly in the quiet atrium adjoining the headquarters complex, "Salve, Caecilius."

"I am glad you see you up and feeling better, my lord general."

"You seem well," observed Antony.

"My soul drank deeply of the pharaoh's wisdom and grace. It is far better than any wine I've ever tasted, even from grapes grown on Vesuvius."

"Pompeii or Herculaneum?" asked Antony.

"Both. My father was born in Pompeii. My mother was born in Herculaneum."

"But you were born in Rome?"

"I was. I spent most of my life in Rome, actually. Then my father fell in battle. He died fighting Caesar on behalf of Pompey."

"I'm sorry to hear that."

"Commoners like me and my family rarely get the luxury of choosing where to serve and how. Like so many he ended up in the wrong legion serving the wrong commanders. Death called him for the simple crime of being in the wrong place at the wrong time.

"When he died I felt I could no longer bear Rome, especially after Pompey's execution. I moved to my uncle's vineyard just outside of Pompeii."

"That is where you gained your reputation for negotiation?"

"Yes! I found myself able to help my uncle's business by talking our way into better deals for both the supplies we needed and the prices we sold our wines at. Profits more than doubled. I am glad I could help them—and you if I am able."

"I wouldn't have anyone else at my side right now. I cannot hope to succeed against the Parthians without money—money the pharaoh possesses that I need."

"Perhaps it would help if I returned to her barge and asked her to come for a banquet tonight?"

"She's refused every other request for such—why would she accept it now?"

"Because we showed humility last night. Maybe you are too hungover to remember, but I was ever at work last night. She thinks well of you, I think, even if you did not make as grand a first impression as you desired."

One hour passed. Dressed in his finest, Caecilius returned to Antony's presence with a bow. Antony met his eyes expectantly, "Well?"

"She has agreed to come here for the promised banquet. She arrives just after sunset," reported Caecilius.

"You have outdone yourself yet again, Caecilius."

"I live to serve!"

"Salve, Caecilius!" smiled Cleopatra as she and her ladies in waiting arrived at atrium in Marc Antony's headquarters.

Caecilius smiled at her and clasped her arms in friendship, as if he were her minister and not Marc Antony's ambassador, "Ave Cleopatrae! Ptolemaeum magna domus!"

"Gratias!" grinned Cleopatra as she released his arms. "You do both your master and Pompeii credit through your service. Yet you are still simply 'Caecilius?' No one has granted you citizenship?"

"I am as common as the bakers of your majesty's bread. I have nothing to offer Rome."

"We will see about that!" declared Cleopatra.

Nodding, Caecilius led the way to Antony and the lavish banquet prepared for Cleopatra.

Stepping inside the room, Cleopatra found Marc Antony much as she spied him from aboard her barge the first time: a soldier of rank and importance, yet a soldier still.

Marc Antony embraced her warmly, "Welcome to my humble abode. I hope you will enjoy yourself tonight. I have planned many entertainments: dancers, acrobats, feats of strength and skill to dazzle the imagination!"

Cleopatra looked at him coolly, "Trying to best me in hospitality then?"

"Well, I am not certain any man, let alone a soldier, can accomplish that. But I will try if you allow me."

"Well then let me see what the best Rome has to offer me entails. So far, I am far more impressed by your servant Caecilius than I am you. Would you consider parting with him?"

"He's not a slave, you know, but a freeman …"

"A freeman without Roman citizenship," countered Cleopatra.

"What would you do with him?"

"Transfer him to my personal staff where he can earn enough money to buy his citizenship —and a sizable home and estate in Pompeii—if he so desires."

"I have no such money to offer him for his services. If you wish to pay him such sums, be my guest."

Cleopatra met his eyes, "At long last, you are learning! It took you long enough!"

Antony sat her down at table, "I am not a man of many words, Your Majesty. Caecilius is the one who knows how to speak well in front of others. I speak better with my gladius and with my legions."

Cleopatra took the offered seat and picked up a cup of wine, "Are you often victorious?"

"Usually—when I have sufficient money to wage my campaigns."

"Which is why you need my patronage."

"Yes."

Cleopatra surveyed the room, "All of this expense so you can impress me to give you money that presently you do not have. Well in one thing at least you have learned from your master Caesar!"

"He was a good man," complemented Antony.

"No, he wasn't," corrected Cleopatra. "He was ruthless and usually unkind. I loved him, yes, but not for his virtues. Those he did not possess. He was vicious, vindictive, and self-serving. He crucified men when a fine would have sufficed. He terrorized and destroyed needlessly. He was a power-driven conqueror."

"I am surprised to hear you speak this way about the man who allegedly was the love of your life."

"Loving someone does not make one blind to their nature. Gaius and I understood one another. We asked of each other only what the other was already prepared to give. There were no lies, no deceptions between us. As for the sex … he possessed more than enough skill and experience to secure from me exactly what he wanted when he wanted it."

"You do not seem easily conquered."

"I am not. Which is why despite all your advances last night you woke up in your bed and I woke up in mine."

"I see …"

"The women you bedded before look up to you. They are easily impressed by your power and your status in Rome. I am not. I wield more power in my own right than all the Roman citizen women combined. Yes, even your wife Fulvia! You know it too! Maybe she obediently goes to your bed when called. I will not."

"I see," fidgeted Antony awkwardly. "Caecilius, what say you on the matter?"

"You are in the presence of greatness, Sire. One would be wise to surrender to her majesty's wit, charms, and intellect," answered Caecilius shrewdly.

"Then surrender I must!" concluded Antony. "Your Majesty, you know what I need and why I need it. What must I do to secure your patronage?"

"First, Caecilius for my court and my government."

"Granted!"

"Second, I want my half-sister Arsinoë dead. While she lives under the protection of the Temple of Artemis in Ephesus she remains a threat to my personal safety and sovereignty."

"That should be easily enough done."

"Third … I want Egypt's power and influence extended across all of the eastern provinces. You want the means to expand the empire and to hold onto the provinces you already have? Then it cannot be by Rome's hand alone. Either this becomes an equal Roman-Egyptian partnership ruled by you and I together or I will simply step back and leave you to your own devices and resources to fend for yourself as you are best able," commanded Cleopatra.

"No wonder you prefer Caecilius' company to my own," mused Antony quietly. "You two have much in common."

"You speak as a man whose vanity has been insulted," observed Cleopatra.

"Indeed, it has been. If I wanted to seduce you tonight I do not think I could accomplish it. You have stolen my prowess for such things with your demands."

"Better an honest rival than a false-friend, Antony. You asked me what I want in order for you to gain what you want. I have answered you truthfully. There is no hidden agenda nor do I think there should be. Alliances based on deceit never endure. Ask anyone among the Aedui in Gaul. They will tell you the same. Rome speaks to Egypt with guile and deceit. It claims we are friends when Octavian has made it clear he regards my kingdom as a client-state. Many Gallic tribes were also client-states—until they were betrayed. My aim is to nullify Rome's ability to treat Egypt as one of its many provinces, to use and abuse as it sees fit. My aim is to secure my throne for myself and my children. In truth would you expect any less of any pharaoh?"

"No, no I would not," answered Antony thoughtfully. "You are perhaps right to demand these things. Nevertheless, I find myself unprepared to make a bargain with you right now. You demand more than I am prepared to give. Yet if I do not comply, the Parthians are likely to overrun these lands and make them their own."

"You have much to think about," agreed Cleopatra.

"I do," conceded Antony.

"Perhaps some wine and good food will help?" suggested Cleopatra.

Marc Antony took her hand and kissed it, "Yes! Perhaps that would help!"

The next morning Marc Antony woke in his bed surprised to see Cleopatra laying naked beside him, the last few hours a complete blur in his head; another hangover pounding through his skull from too much wine and good cheer. Pleased but still completely surprised, Antony caressed her shoulders. Cleopatra purred and faced him, "You look surprised."

"I am."

"You do not remember any of it?"

"No. Did I? Did you? How did it?"

"You agreed to my terms for my patronage. I rewarded you accordingly by giving you what you were most curious to experience."

"Did I ... accomplish my task to your satisfaction?"

"Well enough."

"Well enough for what?"

"For me to allow you the same when you are sober. There are conditions of course."

"Those being?"

"Fidelity."

"Will you promise the same then?"

"No."

"Why not?"

"You have not yet earned it. You are my supplicant, my servant. I am not yours."

"I am a man. You are Aphrodite?"

"Isis, but yes!"

"I agree to your terms."

"Good."

"What now?"

"You romance me throughout Tarsus. You earn my bed while I tarry here. Then I go back to Alexandria. If I am pleased with you, you shall come with me along with whatever staff you wish to accompany you," dictated Cleopatra.

Marc Antony kissed her like an awkward teenager, "I shall obey. Whatever you want, I shall provide."

The next several months passed like a dream for Marc Antony. Pleased at his romancing in Tarsus, Cleopatra invited him to sail away with her back to Alexandria, an offer he could not refuse. Day flowed to night and night flowed into day as Cleopatra shrewdly and apparently happily invited him to her bed—or was that the wine and the many parties in the name of the god Dionysus that followed? A month after arriving in Alexandria, Antony and Cleopatra founded "the Society of Immutable Livers" in Dionysus' name as a place to worship the god and enjoy all His gifts to their fullest.

Happy too was the news that Cleopatra was pregnant. Since she took no one else to her bed, during the parties or outside them, Antony felt confident in his paternity. He wanted to live the rest of his life in Alexandria, taking to his bed Cleopatra and only Cleopatra, and raising his family with her.

It was a beautiful dream—but one that came crashing down before it could be fulfilled.

Chapter Six

"News from Rome, my lord general!" announced Caecilius as he received a dispatch handed to him by one of Antony's soldiers.

Antony rose from his couch lazily, his head still a bit foggy from the meeting of the society of mutable livers the night before, "Read it for me, Caecilius, if you please."

Caecilius broke open the wax seal on the dispatch, "Gaius Julius Caesar Octavianus commands you to return to Rome."

"Why?" asked Antony with annoyance.

"Your wife Fulvia is dead. You are required to perform your duties to her and to her memory as her heir. Moreover, there are other duties that he says you have neglected and are therefore required to perform on behalf," summarized Caecilius. "If you doubt my summary you are welcome to read it for yourself, though in your current state you might find the language difficult to comprehend."

"Octavian wants me back under his control and where he can see me," assessed Marc Antony.

"There is a very high chance of it, yes, my lord general."

"How long can I delay?"

"You cannot. You are ordered to return to Rome with the escort he sent with this dispatch and depart at once," reported Caecilius as he handed the scroll over to Antony to read himself.

Marc Antony opened the scroll and read it, cursing repeatedly under his breath before meeting Caecilius' eyes, "Very well. Ask my aide to pack my belongings. I will return to Rome at once."

Six months passed. Laying back in her bed after successfully and safely delivering a daughter and a son she named Cleopatra and Alexander, Pharaoh Cleopatra breathed a sigh of relief. A knock sounded at the door, "Enter!"

Opening the door for the boy, Caecilius appeared with a smile, the seven-year-old Prince Ptolemy Caesar dragging him into his mother's presence, "Forgive me, my lady! The boy refused to wait!"

Cleopatra smiled at the sight of her eldest son dragging her favourite minister into the room, "No apologies necessary, Caecilius— or should I call you Lobias Caecilius Quintus?"

"My lady?" asked a very confused Caecilius.

"Congratulations, Caecilius! You are officially now a citizen of Rome and entitled to all of the benefits of citizenship—including a proper Roman name," announced Cleopatra with a smile. "I found out just moments before I went into labour. I would have told you before except only my midwives and ladies in waiting are permitted in my presence while I give birth."

Caecilius stammered, "I-I-I understand completely!"

"Do you like the name I chose for you?"

"Almost. If it is not too much trouble I would prefer to be called Lucius Caecilius Lucundus—after my father Lucius."

"Agreed! Lucius Caecilius Lucundus it is!"

Ptolemy Caesar tapped his mother's arm, "Mama, there's a letter for you from Rome!"

"Lucius? Is he right?"

Lucius pulled out the small scroll he slid between his belt and his tunic before entering and handed it to Cleopatra, "Thank you, your highness! I almost forgot!"

Cleopatra opened the scroll, "It's from Marc Antony. He writes that the senate commanded him to remarry at once upon completion of all funerary rites on behalf of Fulvia. Octavian offered him his sister Octavia in matrimony which the senate immediately approved, a match to cement an alliance with Octavian and designed to end the civil war between them. He writes that he does not love her as he loves me, but wedded and subsequently bedded Octavia one week ago. The rest are affirmations of his affection and so forth, his loyalty to me."

"Will you write to him about Cleopatra and Alexander?"

"Yes, but not immediately. He has chosen Rome over Egypt. Despite everything I have given him, he still prefers to rule at Octavian's side than mine. There will be consequences of course. There always is," mused Cleopatra quietly.

"Is there anything I can do for you, Your Majesty?"

"Will you send for the wet nurse to take the twins and see to their needs? I am tired from giving birth and need some sleep."

Lucius Caecilius Lucundus bowed as he took Prince Ptolemy Caesar's hand, "Of course! Come, Your Highness! You must allow your mother to sleep now. You can visit your brother and sister later."

Ptolemy Caesar turned back as Lucius began to escort him out, "Bye, Mama!"

"Good-bye Caesarion," answered Cleopatra as the boy disappeared with Caecilius and sleep swept through her body.

Two years passed in silence. Despite intending to write Antony about their twins, Cleopatra found it wiser to say nothing. After all, what was there to say? She took Marc Antony to her bed because it was politically expedient and promised to secure for her a free and independent Egypt. In giving into Octavian and the senate's demands regarding Octavia, Marc Antony made it clear that he was Rome's ally and not hers. Though she personally liked him and enjoyed their time together, Cleopatra knew she was not in-love with Marc Antony, that her heart still belonged to Gaius Julius Caesar now nine years since his murder. Antony was a bauble to her court and a skilled lover for her bed she found extremely pleasing—but she did not love him. As the months passed, Cleopatra understood at last: her truest and deepest love was for Egypt and for her people, for Alexandria and its unrivalled library system, for learning and wisdom. Men might be fickle and take many lovers to their beds. But Egypt – Egypt was forever. Egypt was faithful to her.

"My lady, Madame, Marc Antony has written to you again," reported Lucius Caecilius Lucundus.

"What does he want?" asked Cleopatra as she watched her children play together.

"He said he will be in Antioch in three weeks and asks you to please join him."

"Why would I want to do that? By all accounts he has two children by his new wife. What does he want with me?"

"Your patronage, I imagine."

"Roman politicians are so fickle," observed Cleopatra. "You, Lucius Caecilius Lucundus are too good a man to continue diplomatic service. You deserve a nice estate in Pompeii, a wife, children, a business."

"My place is with you!" asserted Caecilius.

Cleopatra embraced him warmly, "You are too good a friend, Lucius! Yet I think it is time for us to part. Get married, start your family! Spend the remaining time you have enjoying the rewards of your citizenship. You deserve that."

"If it is that important to you then I will—on one condition."

"Name it!"

"You permit me to return to Pompeii with some flowers and fruit tree saplings to plant in a special garden in your honour," offered Lucius.

"Granted! Take with you whatever you desire and make from these a living memorial to Egypt and these years working together," approved Cleopatra.

"What of Antony's request to see him in Antioch?"

"I will take the twins to see him. Let them look upon their father once in their lifetime."

Three weeks later Pharaoh Cleopatra and twins Cleopatra and Alexander quietly dismounted their camels as they arrived in the metropolis of Antioch, a city nearly as large and grand as her own Alexandria and founded over three hundred years before by another of Alexander the Great's generals—much as her own ancestor Ptolemy I Soter had built Alexandria on behalf of Alexander. Slipping into a quiet villa, Cleopatra rested from the long journey, a journey she knew would have taken less time by sea than by land, but also more conspicuously than traveling with one of the dozens of caravans that routinely travelled between the two cities.

A knock sounded at the door. "Come!" ordered Cleopatra, her eyes widening as Marc Antony entered—without an escort and without fanfare. "This is the second time I have travelled because you asked me to. Tell me, Antony, what is so important that you could not conduct your business with me by proxy?"

Marc Antony took her by the hand and knelt humbly at her feet, "I have a question to ask you which I cannot ask by proxy."

"What question?"

"Cleopatra Thea Philopator, will you marry me?"

"You are already married and have two children by her. Why would I do that?"

"Because I love you and I know you love me, even if you refuse to admit it," asserted Antony.

"A married man may not marry a second wife while the first wife lives. Your Roman law; not ours."

"I have no interest in Octavia."

"Your children by her say otherwise."

"I was a fool to leave you!" asserted Marc Antony. "Please, I beg you! Marry me!"

"One condition."

"Name it!"

"You break with Octavian and cede to me the territories I desire."

"Yes! Yes! Whatever you want! I am yours, Cleopatra! I cannot live without you, not for one more day! Marry me and everything I have, everything that is my power to give I shall give to you —and our children of course."

Cleopatra met his eyes coolly, her mind full of strategy, "Very well. Let it be done and done swiftly—and with formal and legal recognition of your children in the same ceremony."

"There is an eclipse tomorrow. Will that suffice? We will do it during the eclipse, all of it together."

"Very well," agreed Cleopatra. "Until tomorrow night. You are dismissed."

The following night arrived without fanfare. In a simple ceremony Cleopatra presented the twins to their father. In honour of the sun, Antony declared his son was now "Alexander Helios." In honour of the moon he declared his daughter "Cleopatra Selene." Satisfied, Cleopatra consented in front of the priest to be wed to Marc Antony, even if she no longer trusted him. Accepting him to her bed again, Cleopatra tried to enjoy herself as Antony consummated the marriage with her. For three days she allowed him to do what he wanted with her as often as he wanted. With Antony's lust sated, at least for a while, Cleopatra and the twins left Antioch and headed south with another Egyptian caravan. This one headed for Jerusalem.

"What do you mean Cleopatra Thea Philopator is coming here?" asked King Herod nervously, his new palace in Jerusalem still looking more like it belonged to the Hasmonean King Antigonus II Mattathias, the puppet king of the Parthians, than to him. Though officially 'king of the Jews,' Herod remained ever mindful that in the eyes of the people he ruled, he was a foreigner, a puppet hand-picked by Marc Antony to control an unruly and often rebellious Jewish people hell bent on independence from both the Romans and Parthians.

"He means, you should be prepared for my royal presence," declared Cleopatra sternly as she strode up behind him.

Herod barked at her as the aide he was speaking to before slithered away, "How did you get in here so quickly and unannounced?"

"Your staff are incompetent," observed Cleopatra.

"That I know. Why are you here?"

"Because I am pharaoh and I wish to be here. Oh, and one tiny detail: Marc Antony has ceded the eastern provinces to my control."

"Not according to Octavian, he hasn't!" snarled Herod.

"Do you win over many subjects with this attitude, Herod? Based on what I see, the people hate you. You've been their king what? Three years at most?"

"What is it to you?"

"Mismanagement of any province is the business of its overlords. If not for Masada, I doubt either of us would be standing here right now," taunted Cleopatra. "Now, Herod, before this continues and one of us does something she or he will regret for some time, may I suggest you summon your servants and offer me a bit of comfort for myself and my children. We will be staying here in Jerusalem a few days before continuing onwards back to Alexandria with its much more favourable climate."

Herod acquiesced, "Of course!"

Ten days later Cleopatra and her twins departed Jerusalem, satisfied at her success in goading the paranoid idiot king of the Jews. As she arrived back at her palace in Alexandria she found the city ablaze with rumours that Herod plotted to kill her. Other rumours claimed she seduced Herod out of revenge for Marc Antony's marriage to Octavia. No one in Alexandria believed the seduction rumours of course, for such was Herod's reputation already as a vain and untrustworthy manipulator and megalomaniac.

As Antony continued in his largely unsuccessful campaigns against the Parthians, Cleopatra found herself settling back into normal life in Alexandria, her "marriage" to Antony meaning very little to her. Gone were her assumptions that Antony was a trustworthy ally; he could never earn such complete faith in him again as once he possessed. But if marriage is what it took to force Antony to prioritize Egyptian interests, then so be it. Except for that pesky detail that he was also married to Octavia and therefore was a man with two completely opposing loyalties, loyalties Cleopatra knew would be tested.

As the weeks settled into months Cleopatra realized her brief toleration of Antony back in her bed had a new and somewhat unwelcome side effect: she was pregnant again. As summer yielded to autumn and autumn became winter, Cleopatra readied herself to give birth again. This time without the comforting presence of Lucius Caecilius Lucundus to cheer her through her labour.

"It's a boy!" smiled the midwife as Cleopatra screamed in one final burst of strength from her labour.

Panting and feeling weak and exhausted, Cleopatra tried to catch her breath, "Is he healthy?"

"As healthy as a baby can be," glowed the midwife. "Do you know what you wish to call him?"

"Ptolemy Philadelphus," declared Cleopatra as she laid back and let sleep take her blissfully.

Two years of war passed. Though Marc Antony returned to Alexandria and his family there as often as he could, the break between him and Octavian created by his marriage to Cleopatra kept him on the battlefield and away from Egypt for most of the year. In his campaigns against the Parthians on the eastern marches of Asia Minor, Marc

Antony found himself a military failure, the border now less secure than ever. That he could no longer rely upon reinforcements from the rest of the empire did not help. Antony was on his own now with Cleopatra making the day to day decisions on how to govern what Rome claimed as the eastern provinces. Still, he could pretend he was victorious, especially after his unusual luck in winning a key battle in Armenia. But what is victory without a Triumph? Yes! That is what he needed. Perhaps then Cleopatra could forgive him for marrying Octavia and siring his two daughters with her.

Trumpets blared and drums pounded to the rhythm of Roman legionary sandals through the streets of Alexandria. Beginning the Triumphal procession at the Temple of Isis in the alpha quarter of the city, Marc Antony's surviving solders marched south to the public gardens before turning west towards the epsilon quarter, the route taking them past many of the public buildings and temples, including the Temple of Serapis, that made Alexandria world-famous. Reaching the beta quarter, the procession turned east along the city's carefully laid out street grid until it reached the residential gamma quarter before turning north again for its final approach to the gymnasium, its location carefully placed between the Temple of Saturn and the Sun Gate on the border between the alpha and gamma quarters.

Inside the gymnasium's massive courtyard, Cleopatra sat on golden thrones surrounded by her four children on smaller but equally grand thrones. As the procession entered the courtyard at last, the massive and crowded gathering of Alexandrians cheered expectantly. Marc Antony emerged from his solders and strode up through them to the waiting Cleopatra. Antony kneeled before her and kissed her hand, "Your Majesty, I come from Armenia victorious!"

Cleopatra rose from her throne, Antony rising with her, "Marcus Antonius, Egypt welcomes you home!"

The crowd thundered with applause and the stamping of their feet.

"Great pharaoh, I come to you not as a Roman, but as the humble servant to your majesty and to the throne of Egypt! In that service I offer you and Egypt gifts!" declared Marc Antony.

"What gifts would you give Egypt?" asked Cleopatra ceremoniously.

"Ptolemy Caesar, our beloved Caesarion and son of my friend Gaius Julius Caesar, I declare you now the 'King of Kings' and your mother, my sweetest pharaoh let her be called the 'Queen of Kings.' Together you and your mother are the rightful rulers of Egypt, free of Rome. All claims to the kingdom of Egypt by Rome I hereby nullify. Let Egypt stand independent and free! For you, Ptolemy Caesar are the true heir to your father, not this pretender Octavian!

"These are not the only gifts I give. For just as I love you Caesarion as the son of Julius Caesar, so do I also love my sons and daughter by the fairest lady to ever sit upon the throne of Egypt!

"Therefore, I gift to my eldest son Alexander Helios the empires of Armenia, Media, and Parthia. To my younger son, Ptolemy Philadelphus I gift Phoenicia, Syria, and Cilicia. Finally, to my beloved and cherished daughter Cleopatra Selene I gift Cyrenaica and Libya.

"No more shall Rome strangle these southern and eastern lands with its greed and violence. Here, now I make these gifts to you in freedom and in love. May they endure forever!"

Chapter Seven

In Rome, Octavian's response to Marc Antony's "Donations of Alexandria" came swiftly in a form of a declaration of war. In the senate, Marc Antony was stripped of all his powers, titles, and holdings. Adding to the outrage: Marc Antony officially divorced the noble and innocent Octavia, a wife so cherished in the hearts of Roman citizens that she was elevated to the rank of Vestal Virgin and given a humble statue in the Forum in her honour next to Marc Antony's.

The declaration of war came with a word of words as senators aligned themselves either with Octavian or with Marc Antony, each side seeking to discredit the other by claiming its opponent morally and sexually depraved and lacking Roman virtues and decency.

Finally, after two years of harsh political campaigning the declaration of war, it became clear: words and politics would never settle the conflict and reunite Rome. The only way out of this cold civil war was at the end of a gladius —or the prow of a warship. The stage was set for the greatest and most famous sea battle in Roman history: ACTIUM!

"Are you ready to leave for your ship, Your Majesty?" asked Chione, Cleopatra's chief lady-in-waiting.

"Yes—as soon as I read this letter and reply to it," answered Cleopatra.

"Who is it from?"

"An old friend: Lucius Caecilius Lucundus," smiled Cleopatra as she opened the letter and read it.

"What does he say?"

"He has settled in Pompeii! Thanks to the money he saved while working here in the palace he was able to buy a rather sizable estate and vineyard. He is married now and has a son! Everyone is doing well, it seems."

"What wonderful news!"

"He's still political. He writes concerning all the horrible things said about me by Octavian. I am accused of being a seductress and whore … and worse but I will not repeat what he reports. Octavian has been very busy turning Roman citizens against Marc Antony and me. Not that we haven't had our share of defenders, but clearly if we lose a single battle against Octavian we are likely to lose far more than simply a few hundred good men," frowned Cleopatra.

"What will you write him?"

"I change my mind. I will wait until this matter with Octavian is finished. Let us depart at once!"

Cleopatra paced the deck of her royal barge impatiently, wishing she herself could join in battle raging in the Ionian Sea one mile away near the ancient city of Berenike. A cold September wind blew fiercely through her cloak, causing her to shiver. Two fleets consisting of two hundred thirty vessels fought Octavian on her behalf. Marc Antony was on one of them, she knew—but which one? Fires burned, the plumes of smoke rising over the disabled and sinking ships. Were they hers or Octavian's? How could she know?

A small row boat glided up to her barge. Marc Antony emerged in tears and despair. Cleopatra rushed to him, "What happened?"

"We are destroyed! Though we held the greater numbers, Marcus Vipsanius Agrippa, is the better admiral. We didn't stand a chance!" wailed Marc Antony in anger and despair. "I saw good men die—far too many dying to help me get to boat and back to you! I didn't ask it of them! They threw themselves onto the enemy! They demanded I go! For such was their love and loyalty to me! To me! Why to me? What good did I ever do them? Our ships are lost, Cleopatra! Fifty thousand soldiers and sailors! Will even one thousand return home to their families?"

"Did you send the command to retreat and disengage the enemy?" asked Cleopatra firmly and without emotion.

"I think so, yes, maybe," stammered Marc Antony.

Taking charge Cleopatra motioned to the sailor who rowed Antony to her barge, "Order the retreat of all surviving vessels loyal to us. Tell them to do whatever it takes to survive this day. If that means surrender, then surrender. Save as many lives as you can. Those ships who are still sea worthy should rendezvous at our position here. Transfer as many of the wounded as you can to my barge. My physicians will attend them—as will I if I can. I am not as good as my physician is, but I know enough to assist him effectively. Bring them here. We will wait at this position for one hour or for as long as we can safely."

"Yes, Your Majesty!" saluted the sailor happily.

Cleopatra turned her attention back to the shaken Marc Antony, "You have a different wound to attend to. I prescribe strong drink infused with opium. It will make you sleep. After the wounded are attended to I will check on you to see what else is to be done for you—but not before. I have a navy to attend to and my physician must prepare for the more grievously wounded than you seem to be." Cleopatra motioned for her lady-in-waiting Chione to come to her, "Chione, will you see to it personally that lord Antony is given the medicine I prescribe?"

Chione nodded, "Yes, Your Majesty. It will be done exactly as you instruct."

"Thank you, Chione. I know I can count on you!"

Seventy-five minutes later Cleopatra's barge raised anchor and turned its sails for the return voyage back to Alexandria. Thanks to her leadership nearly two thousand sailors and soldiers were able to make it home, many of them saved by her personal assistance below decks nursing the injured and aiding in sometimes delicate but life-saving surgeries thanks to both her intellectual prowess and her ability to speak Egyptian. As her embattled and greatly survived fleet limped back to Egypt, Cleopatra herself showed no emotion, not even sympathy for Marc Antony, her husband of convenience. If Egypt were to survive she must be at her absolute best as a leader. This was no time for sentiment or even wifely affection. The fate of all Egyptians laid in her able hands. But would it be enough against the full might of Rome now firmly against her and with the Roman gods clearly on Octavian's side?

Autumn came to Alexandria and with it the fullness of the harvest. As Egypt and its neighbours in Syria, Parthia, Cilicia, and beyond celebrated nature's bounty and as the survivors of Actium recovered as much of their health and strength as the gods allowed, Cleopatra felt herself waiting on the edge of a desperate battle. For such is the nature of pauses in fighting during great wars. The fighting stops so that soldiers can help their families with the harvest and so that armies need not fight the harsh winter weather. But a pause is different than a peace. Octavian was still at war with Egypt. Though he did not officially claim to be at war with Marc Antony personally, it was more than obvious to everyone in Rome, Egypt, and beyond that this was a very personal fight for both men, just as Julius Caesar's had become against Pompey.

Despite the weight upon her, Cleopatra carried on as best she could to be the best mother and pharaoh she knew how to be.

Cleopatra VII: Egypt's Last Pharaoh

With the spring came Octavian's long expected and long prepared for siege of Alexandria. For four months Octavian and Cleopatra's forces stayed in stalemate. Finally, in late July Marc Antony could bear it no longer. He would meet Octavian in battle—even if it were for the very last time.

Marc Antony climbed to the top of the watchtower, surveying as best he could his defensive force of nearly twelve thousand. Climbing down, he met with the reporting centurion sent to him, "How bad is it?"

"Not as hopeless as it seems, not if the aim is to break the siege. We stand a very good chance at victory," reported the centurion.

"Define victory."

"Freeing the city from Octavian's blockade on the Mediterranean and restoring access to Lake Mareotis to the south."

"Excellent. Does everyone know the strategy we will be using?"

"Yes, Sir! We are ready."

"Then let it begin and let's get this fiendish battle over with!" commanded Antony as he mounted his horse and charged into battle.

Six hours later, Marc Antony rode back to his camp bloody and tired, a look of relief on his face. Heading into his tent he made an offering at his small altar to Horus, "Thank you, oh mighty Horus for this victory! Though it cost us, perhaps there is still hope for Egypt."

Tired and mentally exhausted, Marc Antony collapsed on his bed and fell asleep.

The next morning Marc Antony woke late to the sounds of battle. Startled he put on his armour alone as the sounds closed in on him. Riding his horse fiercely towards the sound, he drew his gladius, preparing for an onslaught. Too late. What remained of his defensive forces was gone. Completely gone. Octavian and Agrippa had out-manoeuvred him. Totally. Completely. Without hope. Knowing that Roman tradition involved his capture followed by a humiliating return to Rome in chains as part of Octavian's triumph and torturous execution (though fortunately not crucifixion), Marc Antony turned his horse back towards Alexandria for one final meeting with the woman he loved, adored, and worshipped.

Night fell. Furtively and much as Cleopatra had done during the civil war with her brother Ptolemy the Thirteenth, Marc Antony slipped unnoticed into the palace. Hiding in the dark spaces between the columns of Cleopatra's bedroom he waited watchfully. Neither Octavian nor the palace staff could know where he was—until he was ready.

One hour later Cleopatra strode into her bedroom and began to undress for bed. Though she did not know where Antony was, she felt no worry. Staying hidden and out of sight was only prudent. Suddenly a face emerged from the columns. Cleopatra covered herself quickly, "Who is there?"

"Someone you have taken to your bed many times," smiled Marc Antony warmly as he closed the distance between them. Sweeping her into his arms, her dress fell between them. Antony looked at her with delight, "I never thought I would see you naked again!"

"Is that why you have come? To claim your perceived rights as a husband?"

"I would love nothing better—except perhaps time to live! But time we no longer have, my beloved! If we linger, Octavian will take us both prisoners and do his worst upon us."

"So, he has informed me via messenger. He promises me amnesty if I will kill you myself."

"And will you?"

"No, I do not believe him."

"That is very wise. You were always wiser than me, my beloved. Though I think now we are at the end, I loved you more sincerely. You were always married to Egypt, not me. Nothing I said or did, not even giving you three more children could change that. For a long time, I pretended you loved me as I love you. But that was never true," confessed Marc Antony.

"I am sorry for that. It was never my intent to hurt you, Marcus."

Antony kissed her palms and caressed her fingers, "I know. Some times you cannot help who you love and who you do not love. I tried to walk in my friend's shoes and found them too big for me. Try as I might, I could never be more than shadow of the great Gaius Julius Caesar!"

"I am sorry."

"There is nothing to forgive. But there is one last thing you can do for me."

"Name it."

"See to it my body is never found."

"I will have you brought to my tomb this very night if you wish."

"I wish it," affirmed Antony as he drew his sword. "Kiss me good-bye, my darling! I love you!"

Cleopatra kissed him passionately, more passionately and more sincerely than she ever felt towards him during the whole of their relationship. Happy at her sudden burst of love, Antony stepped away from her a few paces before falling onto his sword. Cleopatra watched in sadness as the life inside him faded away. Instinctively she held him close to her, his blood spilling across her skin as she comforted him and kissed him until his eyes saw no more.

Keeping her agreement, Cleopatra ordered her servants to discretely remove Antony to her tomb. Washing the blood off her she covered herself in a simple linen dress and slept as best she could.

The next morning, Octavian strode into Cleopatra's bedroom confidently. Cleopatra rose and met his eyes sternly, "What do you want, Octavian?"

"You, of course!" sneered Octavian.

"You are already married. Or is your plan to simply rape me and pretend I seduced you."

"You flatter yourself if you think I want your bed."

"No, Octavian. I simply choose to conform to what you said of me in Rome to sully my reputation. Tell me, is there a single respectable woman who does not call me 'whore' or 'seductress' or worse? Does any Roman citizen believe I am innocent of the charges laid against me?"

"Innocent? You?" mocked Octavian. "Impossible! I would no more demand you for my bed than I would your sons!"

"Here I thought you were *exactly* that sort of man!" mocked Cleopatra. "Boys are your favourite for your bed!"

75

"Only according to the senators and consuls who support you!" countered Octavian.

"Are we to argue politics all day or is there something you actually want?"

"You are coming to Rome with me."

"Marcus Antonius is dead. He fell on his sword. You promised I would keep my throne if Marc Antony died!" accused Cleopatra.

"I changed my mind!"

"I knew you would."

"Well then, when can you be ready to depart?"

"What about my children?"

"What about them?"

"Do I retain custody of them if I come to Rome with you?"

"You talk as if you have any choice in the matter."

"The god Set could learn tricks from you, Octavian!"

Octavian paced for a moment, "Very well. Your three children by Antony shall come back to Rome with me to be raised by my sister Octavia if you so demand."

"I do. And the eldest boys? What will you do to his son Marcus Antonius Antyllus and my son Ptolemy Caesar?"

"I think you know the answer, Cleopatra. They are too dangerous to live. I cannot have a son of Caesar's own body grow up to challenge me, even a bastard like yours."

"Is that your final answer then?"

"Yes."

"Well then … give me three days to prepare. If I am to die in Rome, at least allow me the dignity to die a queen."

"That I will give you—three days to prepare yourself properly and pack whatever belongings you require for your final days on this Earth," vowed Octavian.

"That is all I ask," affirmed Cleopatra. "Now, since I still am pharaoh while I tarry ere in Alexandria, I must insist you withdraw from my palace. Go visit the Alpha Quarter while you wait. You will find the shopping most exquisite and the books in the Serapeum most enlightening!"

"As you wish," bowed Octavian as he began to exit. "But remember: you have three days! No more!"

"Thank you, Octavian!" bowed Cleopatra.

"Is all ready, Chione?" asked Cleopatra as she raised her epiblema over her head to disguise her features.

"All is ready," confirmed Chione.

"My clothes? My regalia?"

"Waiting for us!" affirmed Chione.

Cleopatra mounted her horse, "Well then, let us make haste. We have a long journey ahead!"

Night fell. Tired from riding all day without stopping more than a few minutes to change horses, Cleopatra at long last reached her tomb. Taking a torch, she navigated its narrow corridors through until she reached the main burial chamber. There, on a simple slab of marble laid Marc Antony, his clothing arranged to disguise and cover his wounds. Two ladies waited for Cleopatra who immediately helped her out of her tunic dress and into her royal gown before placing her double crown representing upper and lower Egypt upon her head. Cleopatra opened two cosmetic jars, "Is this ointment I requested?"

"It is," affirmed one of her ladies.

"How swift is the poison?"

"It was not tested," confessed the lady-in-waiting.

"And the asp? Is that ready in case this fails?"

"It is. All is done according to your instructions. If the poisons in these creams fail to kill you, the asp will most certainly finish the job."

"Well then, let us not delay! I will apply this myself, then lay upon my stone bed. When I am dead, you may join me if you wish."

"We will not leave you!" affirmed the lady.

"Chione!" called Cleopatra as she rubbed each cream into the skin on her face, over her chest, and onto her arms.

"Yes, Your Majesty!"

"You will report to Octavian that I am dead – but not until the third day! Until then, return to palace and conduct the household as if I were still there."

"This I shall do!" affirmed Chione. "Good-bye, Your Majesty."

"Good-bye, Chione," replied Cleopatra. Satisfied enough of the creams were now entering her system, Cleopatra walked over to her stone bed and laid down. Her two remaining ladies handed her the royal sceptre and the royal flail that marked her as pharaoh. Calmly Cleopatra waited as the poison worked its way through her system, paralysing her lungs. Cleopatra closed her eyes and saw no more.

Epilogue

"Mistress, is this story true?" asked Synesius of Cyrene as he found his great mentor, Hypatia of Alexandria, among the many aisles of books at the library at the Serapeum.

"Ah, Synesius! You have finished reading!"

"I have, Mistress! It is a most intriguing story. So different from what I heard when I read Plutarch."

"Plutarch was Octavian's man. Never forget that," reminded Hypatia. "Political expedience and the truth are rarely partners. Usually the truth, along with liberty, is the first casualty of war—or ambition. Less than three years after the death of Marc Antony and Cleopatra in Egypt, the senate officially declared Octavian a god, giving him the title 'Caesar Augustus' and making him the first true emperor of Rome.

"What about the children? What happened to them?"

"As you might expect both Marcus Antonius Antyllus and Ptolemy Caesar were beheaded eleven days after Antony and Cleopatra's deaths. However, their three children together were sent into the care of Octavia who raised them as her own. The brothers disappear from history once they arrive in Rome, but Cleopatra Selene prospered. Octavia lived to see Cleopatra Selene married to King Juba the Second of the African kingdoms of Numidia and Mauretania before dying herself at the age of fifty-eight.

"As for Lucius Caecilius Lucundus, he lived long enough to see his namesake grandson born in the year 14. Building upon his grandfather's legacy, the younger Lucius Caecilius Lucundus became a very successful businessman in Pompeii. He died in the year 62 at the age forty-eight during one of the many earthquakes that quietly warned that Vesuvius was awakening from its long slumber, destroying Pompeii and Herculaneum on the twenty-forth of August in the year 79," recounted Hypatia.

"What a tragic story!" remarked Synesius.

Hypatia shook her head, "More tragic is that these books here in Alexandria are the only records that contradict Octavian and those who sought his favour like Plutarch, books no doubt the Patriarch of Alexandria will see burned at the soonest opportunity.

"Remember that tyranny always comes at the expense of the Truth. Never forget that. And above all else, never stop resisting those who offer the most convenient explanations for why things are as they are. Be kind and patient with others, civil in your disagreements. Question everything you see and hear. Verify every story. Seek the Truth and the Truth will find you—if you are wise and if your heart is kind."

Timeline

2575 – 2130 BCE; the Old Kingdom rules over Egypt. Hieroglyphics appears as a formal writing system, mostly for monumental use. Hieratic develops soon after for writing practical documents on papyrus.

c. 2500 BCE; building begins on Stonehenge on the Salisbury plain in Wiltshire.

c. 2000 BCE; building begins on the Temple of Amen-Ra in Karnak, Egypt.

1938 – 1630 BCE; Egypt's Middle Kingdom.

1700 BCE; the Hyksos invade northern Egypt from Canaan and conquers it.

1550 BCE; deposition and expulsion of the Hyksos from Egypt.

1550 – 1075 BCE; Egypt's New Kingdom.

1508 BCE; birth of Queen Hatshepsut to Pharaoh Thutmose I and principal wife Ahmose.

1481 BCE; birth of Thutmose III.

1482 BCE; death of Thutmose I. Thutmose II become pharaoh with his half-sister and wife Hatshepsut.

1479 BCE; death of Pharaoh Thutmose II. Queen Hatshepsut assumes the throne in her step-son's name.

1458 BCE; death of Queen Hatshepsut. Thutmose III invades Canaan. Victory at the Battle of Megiddo wins Thutmose III control over large parts of Canaan. Egyptian cultural and religious expansion begins, including worship of the Egyptian goddess Hathor.

1458 – 1425 BCE; independent reign of Thutmose III.

1300 BCE; Shang Dynasty Chinese begin recording solar and lunar eclipses. First known observation of a supernova is recorded on an oracle bone of tortoise.

1370 BCE – 1330 BCE; reign of Queen Nefertiti.

1279 BCE; birth of Ramses II the Great.

1213 BCE; death of Ramses II the Great.

1200 BCE; Ramses III loses his Canaanite colonies as a severe regional drought sweeps across Egypt, Canaan, Syria, and beyond.

1125 BCE; fire destroys Jaffa, Egypt's last outpost in Canaan.

743 BCE; Assyrian King Tiglath Pileser III uses his newly created full-time, professional army to defeat rival the rival Urartu kingdom.

741 – 738 BCE; Assyrian siege and conquest of the Syrian kingdom of Arpad.

676 BCE; Assyrian invasion of Egypt.

671 BCE; Assyrian King Esarhaddon captures and destroys the Egyptian capitol of Memphis.

612 BCE; fall of the Assyrian Empire. Egypt regains independence.

600 BCE; Demotic script replaces hieratic as the main form of written Egyptian. Hieratic becomes the script of Egyptian religious writing until finally falling out of favour during the Ptolemaic Dynasty.

c. 580 BCE; birth of King Cyrus II the Great in Persis, Iran.

550 BCE; Cyrus II ascends the Persian throne and begins a war of conquest of first the nearby Medes, then the Babylonians. Birth of Darius the Great.

547 BCE; Cyrus II conquers the Lydian kingdom of Croesus.

539 BCE; Cyrus the Great conquers the Babylonian Empire. Soon after he gives permission for 40,000 Jews to leave Babylon and return to Palestine.

529 BCE; death of Cyrus the Great. Cyrus's eldest son Cambyses ascends the Persian throne as King Cambyses II.

525 BCE; Persian King Cambyses II conquers Egypt.

522 BCE; King Cambyses II dies under mysterious circumstances. After several weeks of turmoil, Cambyses' cousin Darius ascends the throne as Darius I the Great.

486 BCE; death of Darius the Great.

366 BCE; Greek noblewoman Arsinoe gives birth to Ptolemy Soter. Though claimed by Macedonian nobleman Lagus, it is believed Arsinoe was one of King Philip II of Macedonia's many mistresses and Ptolemy one of Philip II's illegitimate sons.

333 BCE, November; Battle of Issus in Syria. Alexander the Great defeats Persian King Darius III Codomannus to win Phoenicia and Egypt from the Persians.

330 BCE; Alexander the Great founds the city of Alexandria and makes it the new Egyptian capitol.

324 BCE; Ptolemy Soter marries Artacama, the daughter of Persian courtier Artabazus.

323 BCE; Alexander puts (his half-brother) General Ptolemy Soter in charge of Egypt to rule as its governor.

318 BCE; Ptolemy Soter sends Artacama into exile to make room for his second wife, Bernice I of Egypt.

316 BCE; birth of Arsinoe Philadelphus to Ptolemy I Soter and Bernice I of Egypt.

305 BCE; Ptolemy Soter assumes the title of king and pharaoh to become Ptolemy I Soter.

c. 305 BCE; Pharaoh Ptolemy I creates the cult of Serapis to unify Greeks and Egyptians together under one religion with worship integrating beliefs and imagery from both cultures.

c. 295 BCE; exiled Athenian Governor Demetrius of Phalerum organizes construction of the "Temple of the Muses" (Musaeum) complex as a library and centre of intellectual discourse and learning. The library's collections grow so large that two sister libraries are built to house more books and provide more classrooms to educators. Collectively the library system becomes known as "the Great Library of Alexandria."

290 BCE; Ptolemy I Soter elevates his wife Bernie I to "Queen of Egypt."

299 BCE; Ptolemy marries his daughter Arsinoe off to Lysimachus of Thrace.

281 BCE; death of Lysimachus of Thrace.

282 BCE; death of Pharaoh Ptolemy I Soter. Eldest daughter Arsinoe II Philadelphus becomes Pharaoh.

275 BCE; Pharaoh Arsinoe II marries her full brother Ptolemy II Philadelphus.

270 BCE; Death of Arsinoe Philadelphus.

238 BCE; Ptolemy III Euergetes makes the Canopus Decree which defies his daughter Berenice with a provision for a new calendar with 365 days and an extra day added every four years. The calendar is rejected.

Cleopatra VII: Egypt's Last Pharaoh

218-201 BCE; Second Punic War brings Rome to prominence in the Mediterranean region.

200 BCE; at the Battle of Panium, Pharaoh Ptolemy V Epiphanes loses Asia Minor and Palestine to the Seleucid kings of Syria.

140 BCE; birth of Ptolemy X Alexander I.

132-134 BCE; civil war against Pharaoh Ptolemy VIII ravages the city of Alexandria.

118 BCE; resolution of the Egyptian civil war.

117 BCE; birth of Ptolemy XII to Ptolemy IX and an unknown mother.

116 BCE; Ptolemy IX Soter II becomes ruler of Egypt.

105 BCE; birth of Ptolemy XI Alexander.

103 BCE; Ptolemy X invades Judea after involving himself and Egypt in the Hasmonaean civil war.

100 BCE July 12; birth of Gaius Julius Caesar* in Rome to Gaius Julius Caesar (senior) and Aurelia Cotta.

88 BCE; After being deposed (once more) by Pharaoh Ptolemy IX and exiled from Egypt, Pharaoh Ptolemy X Alexander dies trying to invade Cyprus; bequeaths Egypt to Rome.

84 BCE; death of Gaius Julius Caesar (senior). Gaius Julius Caesar succeeds his father as head of the family. In pursuit of the high priesthood of Jupiter which would afford him greater wealth and power, Julius Caesar marries Cornelia, the daughter of influential patrician Lucius Cinna.

82 BCE; Lucius Cornelius Sulla declares him Dictator of Rome. Targeted by Sulla's political purges, Julius Caesar is stripped of his priesthood and his wife's dowry leaving him and his wife penniless. Needing an income, Julius Caesar joins the army.

81 BCE; death of Ptolemy IX.

79 BCE; death of Sulla. Julius Caesar returns to Rome.

76 BCE; birth of Berenice IV to Pharaoh Ptolemy XII Auletes and Cleopatra VI Tryphaena.

75 BCE; Cornelia gives birth to Julia Caesaris. Birth of Calpurnia to Lucius Calpurnius Piso Caesoninus.

69 BCE; Cleopatra VII Thea Philopator is born to King Ptolemy XII and his sister Queen Cleopatra V Tryphaena. Death of Cornelia in Rome; Gaius Julius Caesar becomes a widower. Birth of Octavia to Gaius Octavius and his second wife Atia.

67 BCE; Gaius Julius Caesar marries Pompeia, the granddaughter of Roman dictator Sulla.

65 BCE; Ptolemy XII Auletes throws his support behind Pompey. In Rome, the Senate discusses annexing Egypt.

64 BCE; Rome annexes Syria's Seleucid Empire.

63 BCE; with the help of Pompey the Great and Marcus Licinius Crassus, Caesar becomes Pontifex Maximus of Rome. Pompey conquers Judea.

63 BCE, 23 September; birth of Gaius Octavius (Octavian).

62 BCE; Caesar divorces Pompeia following a scandal involving another man. Caesar is elected praetor.

61 BCE; birth of Ptolemy XIII. Caesar takes up the governorship of Hispania where he defeats the warring Celtic tribes of the province.

60 BCE; Caesar begins his wars of conquest across Gaul and Germania.

58 BCE; Lucius Calpurnius Piso Caesoninus becomes consul. Daughter Calpurnia catches Caesar's eye as a possible politically advantageous match.

59 BCE; Caesar marries his third wife Calpurnia and remains married to her for the rest of his life. Ptolemy XII Auletes promises Pompey and Caesar 6000 talents. Rome responds by declaring Ptolemy XII "an ally and friend of the Roman Nation."

58 BCE; Caesar invades Gaul and begins his long series of conquests of the continental Celtic speaking peoples from the west bank of the Rhine through modern France and into modern Spain. Rome annexes Cyprus. Riots in Alexandria forces Ptolemy XII into exile. Ptolemy's eldest daughter Berenice IV takes control over Egypt.

57 BCE; Caesar conquers the Belgic tribes of northeast Gaul. Fulvia gives birth to daughter Claudia (Clodia Pulchra) by her first husband Publius Clodius Pulcher.

55 BCE; Ptolemy XII Auletes returns to Alexandria. Berenice IV deposed and killed.

52 BCE; Caesar defeats the Gallic war leader Vercingetorix at the Battle of Alesia. Gaul falls into complete and permanent Roman control and domination.

51 BCE; Ptolemy XII dies, leaving his throne to Cleopatra and Ptolemy. In accordance with Egyptian custom, Cleopatra and Ptolemy marry in order to rule over Egypt. Due to Ptolemy's minority the eunuch Pothinus is appointed regent over him.

49 BCE, 10-11 January; Caesar leads his troops across the Rubicon River. Beginning of civil war between Caesar and Pompey.

48 BCE Spring-Summer; key Egyptian court officials Pothinus, Achillas, and Theodotus plot to remove Cleopatra from the throne and make Ptolemy XIII sole ruler of Egypt. In the ensuing civil war, Cleopatra flees Egypt to Syria. Battle of Pharsalus in Greece between Caesar and Pompey. Defeated by Caesar's army, Pompey the Great flees to Egypt.

48 BCE Summer - Autumn; Cleopatra returns to Egypt from Syria with an army. Battle of Pelusium. Chinese record a supernova; its remnant is believed to be SNR 021.5-00.9.

48 BCE Autumn; Pompey abandons Italy and flees to Egypt with Caesar in pursuit. Caesar battles Ptolemy on behalf of Cleopatra.

47 BCE; Battle of the Nile between Ptolemy XIII and Gaius Julius Caesar. Ptolemy XIII drowns in the Nile fleeing Caesar's army. Younger brother Ptolemy XIV becomes Cleopatra's husband. Caesar pens "Veni, Vidi, Vici" after defeating Pharnaces II of Pontus at the Battle of Zela. Gaius Julius Caesar returns to Rome and holds all four of his Triumphs saved up over the years at once. As part of the celebrations, Vercingetorix is paraded in chains before being quietly strangled to death. In Egypt Cleopatra gives birth to Julius Caesar's son, Ptolemy Caesar who is quickly nicknamed "Caesarion."

46 BCE; Cleopatra and Caesarion arrive in Rome at Caesar's invitation. Caesar provides a villa for them for their stay which he visits frequently. Caesar places a statue of Cleopatra in the Temple of Venus in Rome.

44 BCE; Marc Antony marries Fulvia daughter of Marcus Fulvius Bambalio of Tusculum and mother (by her first marriage to Publius Clodius Pulcher) to Claudia, wife of Octavian.

44 BCE, March; with rumours flying of a possible assassination plot against him, Gaius Julius Caesar dismisses his body board in a show of confidence in his ability to survive. Calpurnia dreams about Caesar's murder. Caesar seeks counsel from a soothsayer who confirms the validity of Calpurnia's vision and urges him to stay home until the danger passed.

44 BCE, 14 March; Caesar joins some friends for dinner. During the discussion Caesar declares that "sudden death" is the best way to die.

44 BCE 15 March; assassination Gaius Julius Caesar at the Theatre of Pompey. In his will, Gaius Julius Caesar names great nephew Octavian as his adopted son and heir, renaming him Gaius Julius Caesar Octavianus.

44 BCE, spring; In the aftermath of Caesar's murder, Cleopatra leaves Rome and returns to Egypt with Caesarion.

42 BCE; the Roman senate deifies Gaius Julius Caesar. Octavian marries Fulvia's daughter Claudia.

41 BCE Spring; Marc Antony summons Cleopatra to Tarsus. Over the winter Cleopatra becomes pregnant by Antony.

40 BCE; death of Marc Antony's first wife Fulvia. Octavian divorces Fluvia's eldest daughter Claudia. Marc Antony and Cleopatra establish the "Society of Inimitable Livers" dedicated to the worship of Dionysus. Marc Antony marries Octavian's sister Octavia. Cleopatra gives birth to twins Alexander Helios and Cleopatra Selene.

39 BCE, August; Octavia gives birth to Marc Antony's daughter Antonia the Elder.

37 BCE; Antony summons Cleopatra and the twins to Antioch in Syria where he formally recognizes them as his children. Antony and Cleopatra marry. Beginning of open rivalry with Octavian Caesar.

36 BCE; birth of Ptolemy Philadelphus to Antony and Cleopatra.

36 BCE, 31 January; Octavia gives birth to Marc Antony's youngest daughter Antonia the Younger.

34 BCE; in a grand ceremony called "the Donations of Alexandria" Marc Antony declares Caesarion "King of Kings" and Cleopatra "Queen of Kings."

32 BCE; Marc Antony divorces Octavia.

31 BCE, 2 September; Octavian Caesar defeats Marc Antony and Cleopatra's fleet at the Battle of Actium.

30 BCE, 31 July; Marc Antony defeats Octavian at the Battle of Alexandria.

30 BCE 12 August; Marc Antony and Cleopatra commit suicide in Alexandria. Octavian takes Marc Antony's three children back to Rome as trophies. Marc Antony's ex-wife Octavia takes Antony and Cleopatra's children into her home and raises them with her own children. All of Cleopatra's wealth is confiscated and becomes such a major boost to the Roman economy that the standard interest rate drops from 12% to 4%.

30 BCE, 23 August; Octavian executes Cleopatra's son Ptolemy Caesar (fathered by Gaius Julius Caesar), and Marc Antony's son by his first Roman wife Fulvia, Marcus Antonius Antyllus.

27 BCE; Octavian Caesar is made the first Roman Emperor and proclaimed "Caesar Augustus."

11 BCE; death of Octavian's sister Octavia.

14 CE; birth of Lucius Caecilius Lucundus in Pompeii.

14 CE, 23 September; death of Octavian (Caesar Augustus).

62 CE, 5 February; death of Lucius Caecilius Lucundus in the aftermath of an earthquake.

79 CE, 24 August; Mount Vesuvius erupts, burying the cities of Herculaneum and Pompeii in ash. Lucius Caecilius Lucundus' business records are preserved in his house.

500 CE; last known use of Egyptian demotic script.

1607 CE; first performance of William Shakespeare's "Antony and Cleopatra."

1963 CE; the epic biographical film "Cleopatra" starring Elizabeth Taylor and Richard Burton revives modern interest in Cleopatra's life and times.

Note: Though most people treat "Caesar" as the family name, the family name is actually Julius Caesar. Gaius is the personal name, not Julius.

Suggested Reading and Bibliography

<u>CLEOPATRA</u>

History.com: Cleopatra

http://www.history.com/topics/ancient-history/cleopatra

History.com: Ten Little Known Facts about Cleopatra

https://www.history.com/news/10-little-known-facts-about-cleopatra

The History of Cleopatra

http://www.historyworld.net/wrldhis/PlainTextHistories.asp?historyid=aa25

Cleopatra VII: Queen

https://www.biography.com/people/cleopatra-vii-9250984

Britannica: Cleopatra, Queen of Egypt

https://www.britannica.com/biography/Cleopatra-queen-of-Egypt

Who Was the Most Powerful Woman in Ancient History?

https://news.nationalgeographic.com/2018/03/powerful-women-ancient-history-cleopatra-artemisia-enheduanna-egypt-greece-mesopotamia/

Has the Hidden Location of the Tomb of Cleopatra Finally Been Found?

http://www.ancient-origins.net/ancient-places-africa/has-hidden-location-tomb-cleopatra-finally-been-found-005304

Egyptian Alexandria - Ancient underwater finds revealed the Pharaonic roots of the Ptolemaic City

http://www.ancient-origins.net/ancient-places-africa/egyptian-alexandria-ancient-underwater-pharaonic-roots-020212

EgyptRevealed.com -- Cleopatra's Sunken Palace

http://www.virtual-egypt.com/newhtml/articles/Cleopatra's%20Sunken%20Palace.htm

Ptolemy XII Auletes

http://www.livius.org/articles/person/ptolemy-xii-auletes/

Cleopatra VII's Childhood and Ptolemy XII

http://kingtutone.com/queens/cleopatra/child/

Cleopatra VII: Egypt's Last Pharaoh

Ptolemy XIII Theos Philopator

https://www.ancient.eu/Ptolemy_XIII_Theos_Philopator/

The Timeline of the Life of Cleopatra

http://www.sjsu.edu/faculty/watkins/cleopatra.htm

Cleopatra

http://penelope.uchicago.edu/~grout/encyclopaedia_romana/miscellanea/cleopatra/cleopatra.html

The Faces of Cleopatra and Antony's Twin Babies Revealed

https://www.livescience.com/19838-antony-cleopatra-babies-sculpture.html

The final resting place of King Juba II & Queen Cleopatra Selene II

https://www.thevintagenews.com/2016/11/08/the-final-resting-place-of-king-juba-ii-queen-cleopatra-selene-ii/

Juba II: King of Numidia And Mauretania

https://www.britannica.com/biography/Juba-II

Aziz, Sofia. "An Examination of the Death of Cleopatra and the Serpent in Myth, Magic and Medicine." *Nile Magazine,* no. 12 (2018). Accessed 18 April, 2018.
https://www.academia.edu/36416885/An_Examination_of_the_Death_of_Cleopatra_and_the_Serpent_in_Myth_Magic_and_Medicine

Taylor, Elizabeth. *Cleopatra*. DVD. Directed and written by Joseph L. Mankiewicz. Los Angeles: Twentieth-Century Fox Film Corporation, 1963.

JULIUS CAESAR

Julius Caesar: Dictator, General

https://www.biography.com/people/julius-caesar-9192504

Ancient.eu: Julius Caesar

https://www.ancient.eu/Julius_Caesar/

Britannica: Julius Caesar, Roman Ruler

https://www.britannica.com/biography/Julius-Caesar-Roman-ruler

Tony Robinson's Romans: Julius Caesar

Part 1: https://youtu.be/3duE5TzSWco

Part 2: https://youtu.be/SOgDbXBDRNo

What Happened to Calpurnia After Julius Caesar's Assassination?

https://www.quora.com/What-happened-to-Calpurnia-after-Julius-Caesar-assassination

Augustus, Roman Emperor

https://www.britannica.com/biography/Augustus-Roman-emperor

Timeline of the Life of Octavian, Caesar Augustus.

http://www.applet-magic.com/caesaraugustus.htm

Strass, Barry. *The Death of Julius Caesar.* New York: Simon and Shuster, 2016.

MARC ANTHONY

Cleopatra Seduces Antony

http://www.eyewitnesstohistory.com/cleopatra.htm

Britannica: Mark Antony, Roman Triumvir

https://www.britannica.com/biography/Mark-Antony-Roman-triumvir

History: Mark Antony

https://www.history.com/topics/ancient-history/mark-antony

Marc Antony Meets Cleopatra

https://www.biography.com/people/groups/mark-antony-and-cleopatra

Antony and Cleopatra: A One-Sided Love Story?

https://medium.com/@FrancisFlisiuk/antony-and-cleopatra-a-one-sided-love-story-d6fefd73693d

Mark Antony Biography

http://www.notablebiographies.com/Lo-Ma/Mark-Antony.html

Plutarch, "The Parallel Lives," The Life of Antony

http://penelope.uchicago.edu/Thayer/E/Roman/Texts/Plutarch/Lives/Antony*.html

Britannica: Fulvia, Wife of Marc Antony

https://www.britannica.com/biography/Fulvia-wife-of-Mark-Antony

Octavia, Wife of Marc Antony

https://www.britannica.com/biography/Octavia-wife-of-Mark-Antony

Unraveling History: The Final Fates of the Children of Cleopatra VII?

https://www.ancient-origins.net/history-famous-people/unraveling-history-final-fates-children-cleopatra-vii-005230

Cleopatra and Antony

https://www.ancient.eu/article/197/cleopatra--antony/

Antony and Cleopatra

http://penelope.uchicago.edu/~grout/encyclopaedia_romana/miscellanea/cleopatra/alma-tadema.html

Ancient Egypt Online: Cleopatra and Marc Antony

https://www.ancientegyptonline.co.uk/Cleopatra-Mark-Antony.html

Octavia Minor: Sister of Augustus, wife of Mark Antony, and great-grandmother of Caligula

https://www.thevintagenews.com/2017/07/10/octavia-minor-sister-of-augustus-wife-of-mark-antony-and-great-grandmother-of-caligula/

Badass Women of History--Octavia the Younger

https://steemit.com/history/@stephmckenzie/badass-women-of-history-octavia-the-younger

Rome - From Republic to Empire: Octavian vs Mark Antony

Part 1 https://youtu.be/8BZyZ-__6z4

Part 2 https://youtu.be/f9zJVzTrnKI

ROMAN EMPIRE

Ancient Rome 101: National Geographic

https://youtu.be/GXoEpNjgKzg

Britannica: Sulla

https://www.britannica.com/biography/Sulla

Exquisitely Designed 2,000-Year-Old Roman Shoe Discovered in a Well

https://mymodernmet.com/womens-shoes-ancient-rome/

Archaeologists Virtually Recreate House of Caecilius Lucundus in Pompeii

http://www.sci-news.com/archaeology/house-caecilius-iucundus-pompeii-04248.html

The House of Lucius Caecilius Lucundus

https://vimeo.com/185534416

Ancient Merchant Banking – the House of Lucius Caecilius Jucundus – the Banker of Pompeii

https://www.armstrongeconomics.com/history/ancient-economies/ancient-merchant-banking-the-house-of-lucius-caecilius-jucundus-the-banker-of-pompeii/

Who were Roman Citizens?

https://rome.mrdonn.org/citizens.html

Development of Roman Citizenship

https://romancitizenshiprights.weebly.com/how-to-gain-or-lose-citizenship.html

The Roman-Parthian War 58-63 CE

https://www.ancient.eu/article/1198/the-roman-parthian-war-58-63-ce/

Roman-Parthian Wars

https://youtu.be/VChHK2X4aI4

The Roman and Parthian Wars

http://www.setterfield.org/Roman-Parthian_Wars.html

Rockefeller, Laurel A. *Boudicca, Britain's Queen of the Iceni*. Pennsylvania: Laurel A. Rockefeller Books, 2014.

Rockefeller, Laurel A. *Hypatia of Alexandria*. Pennsylvania: Laurel A. Rockefeller Books, 2017.

PTOLEMAIC DYNASTY

Arsinoe II Philadelphus (C. 316–270 BCE)

https://www.encyclopedia.com/women/encyclopedias-almanacs-transcripts-and-maps/arsinoe-ii-philadelphus-c-316-270-bce

Ptolemy I

https://www.ancient.eu/Ptolemy_I/

Ptolemaic Dynasty

https://www.ancient.eu/Ptolemaic_Dynasty/

Ptolemy I Soter

http://www.livius.org/articles/person/ptolemy-i-soter/

Britannica: Ptolemy I Soter

https://www.britannica.com/biography/Ptolemy-I-Soter

Lysimachus, King of Macedonia

https://www.britannica.com/biography/Lysimachus

Cleopatra's Egypt

https://youtu.be/fX1CFsaCcW8

Ptolemy VIII

http://www.tyndalehouse.com/egypt/ptolemies/ptolemy_viii_fr.htm

Ptolemy X Alexander

http://www.livius.org/articles/person/ptolemy-x-alexander/

Ptolemy XIV

http://www.livius.org/articles/person/ptolemy-xiv/

Berenice IV

http://www.livius.org/articles/person/berenice-iv/?

Alexandria Through the Ages

https://st-takla.org/Alexandria-1.html

The Economy of Ptolemaic Egypt

https://www.ancient.eu/article/1256/the-economy-of-ptolemaic-egypt/

<u>ANCIENT EGYPT</u>

Odd Facts You Didn't Know about the Ancient Egyptians

https://www.youtube.com/watch?v=J77VI_TUsMk

Ancient Egypt 101 | National Geographic

https://youtu.be/hO1tzmi1V5g

Britannica: Hieratic Script Writing System

https://www.britannica.com/topic/hieratic-script

Britannica: Demotic Script Writing System

https://www.britannica.com/topic/demotic-script

Ancient Egypt: Life and Death in the Valley of the Kings

Part One, Life: https://youtu.be/q_WniaCQ8Iw

Part Two, Death: https://www.youtube.com/watch?v=PI1Ot9ed6vA

Egyptian Kings (Pharaohs), Governors, and Other Rulers.

http://www.touregypt.net/kings.htm

Jewish God Yahweh Originated in Canaanite Vulcan, Says New Theory

https://www.haaretz.com/archaeology/.premium.MAGAZINE-jewish-god-yahweh-originated-in-canaanite-vulcan-says-new-theory-1.5992072

Hathor and the Mines of Timna

http://sidneyrigdon.com/drb/begin/mines.htm

15 Major Ancient Egyptian Gods and Goddesses You Should Know About

https://www.realmofhistory.com/2018/01/16/15-ancient-egyptian-gods-goddesses-facts/

Ancient Egypt: Mining

http://www.reshafim.org.il/ad/egypt/timelines/topics/mining.htm

Egypt Relations with Canaan

http://etc.ancient.eu/interviews/egyptian-relations-canaan/

Ramses II

https://www.ancient.eu/Ramesses_II/

Nefertiti

https://www.history.com/topics/ancient-history/nefertiti

Thutmose III

https://www.ancient.eu/Thutmose_III/

Hatshepsut

https://www.ancient.eu/hatshepsut/

Biography: Hatshepsut

https://www.biography.com/people/hatshepsut-9331094

Egypt's Lost Queens

https://youtu.be/ClX9mQ5n5qI

Royal Titles for Kings of Egypt

http://www.touregypt.net/featurestories/titles.htm

Ancient Egyptian Kings and Queens

https://discoveringegypt.com/ancient-egyptian-kings-queens/

Egypt Uncovered

https://youtu.be/KuUMe-43A3E

The Temple of Serapis in Alexandria

http://penelope.uchicago.edu/~grout/encyclopaedia_romana/greece/paganism/serapeum.html

Ancient Gymnasium Found in Egypt

http://www.socialstudiesforkids.com/articles/currentevents/egypt-ancientgymnasium.htm

Egyptian Symbols and Their Meanings

http://mythologian.net/egyptian-symbols-meanings/

PERSIAN EMPIRE

Encyclopaedia Britannica: Cambyses II, King of Persia

https://www.britannica.com/biography/Cambyses-II

Encyclopaedia Britannica: Darius the Great

https://www.britannica.com/biography/Darius-I

Encyclopaedia Britannica: Cyrus the Great

https://www.britannica.com/biography/Cyrus-the-Great

History of Iran: Cyrus the Great

http://www.iranchamber.com/history/cyrus/cyrus.php

Engineering an Empire: the Persians

https://youtu.be/q49SxV84qec

Achaemenid Dynasty

http://www.iranicaonline.org/articles/achaemenid-dynasty

ASSYRIAN EMPIRE

Assyrian Warfare

https://www.ancient.eu/Assyrian_Warfare/

Egypt and the Assyrians

http://www.ethanholman.com/history/egypt/othercultures/assyrians.
html

HELLENISTIC EGYPT

Britannica: Serapis

https://www.britannica.com/topic/Serapis

What happened to the Great Library at Alexandria?

http://www.ancient.eu/article/207/

The Burning of the Library of Alexandria

https://ehistory.osu.edu/articles/burning-library-alexandria

The Mysterious Fate of the Great Library of Alexandria

http://jameshannam.com/library.htm

The Great Library of Alexandria

http://penelope.uchicago.edu/~grout/encyclopaedia_romana/greece/paganism/library.html

The Library of the Serapeum

http://penelope.uchicago.edu/~grout/encyclopaedia_romana/greece/paganism/daughter.html

Sacred Destinations: the Serapeum

http://www.sacred-destinations.com/egypt/alexandria-serapeum

The Caesareum of Alexandria: Scene of Crime

http://www.cosmographica.com/spaceart/alexandria/caesareum.html

It's All Greek To Me – The Complicated Story of Hanukkah

http://blogs.timesofisrael.com/its-all-greek-to-me-the-complicated-story-of-hanukkah/

Hanukkah Part I, The Ptolemaic Empire

https://youtu.be/54flSoFxKI0

Ptolemy I Soter: Macedonian King of Egypt

https://www.britannica.com/biography/Ptolemy-I-Soter

Ptolemy II Philadelphus: Macdoniam King of Egypt

https://www.britannica.com/biography/Ptolemy-II-Philadelphus

History.com: Cleopatra

http://www.history.com/topics/ancient-history/cleopatra

GREEK SPIRITUALITY AND MYTHOLOGY

Greek Mythology Gods and Goddesses Documentary

https://youtu.be/-MSEsh6jgHE

Eileithyia

http://www.theoi.com/Ouranios/Eileithyia.html

Prometheus

http://www.theoi.com/Titan/TitanPrometheus.html

Britannica: Hesiod

https://www.britannica.com/biography/Hesiod

Hesiod: Theogony (full text)

http://chs.harvard.edu/CHS/article/display/5289

Pandora

http://www.theoi.com/Heroine/Pandora.html

The Earth Mother Rules

http://manicscribbler.blogspot.co.uk/2017/06/the-earth-mother-rules-guest-author.html

Britannica: Serapis

https://www.britannica.com/topic/Serapis

The Cult of Dionysos

http://www.cndp.fr/archive-
musagora/dionysos/dionysosen/culte.htm

Dionysos Cult 1

http://www.theoi.com/Cult/DionysosCult.html

The Cult of Dionysus: Legends and Practice

http://www.greektheatre.gr/dionysian-origins/cult-dionysus/

Cult of Dionysus

https://www.stmuhistorymedia.org/cult-of-dionysus/

Explorations of Dionysus: Cult, Myth, Mystery

https://www.adf.org/articles/gods-and-spirits/hellenic/dionysus.html

Dionysus, Cult of

https://www.jewishvirtuallibrary.org/dionysus-cult-of

GREEK HISTORY, LANGUAGE, AND GEOGRAPHY

Greece: Secrets of the Past

http://www.historymuseum.ca/cmc/exhibitions/civil/greece/gr0000e.shtml

Greece: Daily Life

http://www.historymuseum.ca/cmc/exhibitions/civil/greece/gr1150e.shtml

Greece: Alphabets and Writing

http://www.historymuseum.ca/cmc/exhibitions/civil/greece/gr1060e.shtml

How to Address Your Teacher

https://harzing.com/publications/white-papers/how-to-address-your-teacher

Ancient Greek Names

https://tekeli.li/onomastikon/Ancient-World/Greece/Male.html

How to be polite in Greek

https://blogs.transparent.com/greek/how-to-be-polite-in-greek/

Behind the Name: Hypatia

https://www.behindthename.com/name/hypatia

Acropolis Hill

http://www.greeka.com/attica/athens/athens-excursions/acropolis.htm

Ancient Greek Female Names

http://monsaventinus.wikia.com/wiki/Ancient_Greek_Female_Names_(Greek_Community)

Athens Geography

http://www.greeka.com/attica/athens/athens-geography.htm

Socratic Method

https://www.law.uchicago.edu/socratic-method

Critical Thinking Community: Socratic Method

http://www.criticalthinking.org/pages/socratic-teaching/606

OTHER RESOURCES

Latin Lesson #4

http://www.novaroma.org/aquila/april05/08.htm

Latin Greetings

https://blogs.transparent.com/latin/latin-greetings/

A New Life for the House of Caecilius

https://houseofcaecilius.com/

NASA: A Brief History of High-Energy Astronomy: Before Common Era (BCE)

https://heasarc.gsfc.nasa.gov/docs/heasarc/headates/earlier.html

Explorable: Chinese Astronomy

https://explorable.com/chinese-astronomy

Bible Gateway

https://www.biblegateway.com/passage/?search=Colossians+2&version=NIV

Ancient Greek Clothing

https://www.ancient.eu/article/20/ancient-greek-clothing/

Ancient Greek Clothing - What Did the Ancient Greeks Wear?

http://www.historyofclothing.com/clothing-history/ancient-greek-clothing/

The Quadrant and the Sextant

http://www.sites.hps.cam.ac.uk/starry/quadrant.html

Sirius: The Luminous Star and Ancient Egypt

https://www.gaia.com/article/star-sirius-and-egypt

Hasmonaeans

http://www.livius.org/articles/dynasty/hasmonaeans/?

Reign of Herod the Great: 47 B.C. to his death in 4 B.C.

http://theos-sphragis.info/herods_regnal_years.html

Top 10 Famous Clothes of Ancient Greece

https://www.ancienthistorylists.com/greek-history/top-10-famous-clothes-ancient-greece/

About This Series

The Legendary Women of World History Series was first created in March 2014 in response to poor performance to a simple survey question asking people to name five women from across history whose lives still touch ours today. When less than 10% of the 50-100 people surveyed could name just five and less than 5% could name ten, author and historian Laurel A. Rockefeller decided to take action. The result was this author's best-selling narrative biography, "Boudicca, Britain's Queen of the Iceni" which came to audiences in audio edition in September of the same year.

In May 2015 work began on adapting the Legendary Women of World History Series into a stage drama series. The goal of the Legendary Women of World History Drama Series is both educational and entertainment, bringing the compelling stories of inspiring women to audiences while simultaneously offering commanding lead roles to actresses and offering educational settings enhanced opportunities working with the challenges of period dramas.

Today you can find the Legendary Women of World History Series and Legendary Women of World History Drama Series in English, French, Spanish, Chinese, Italian, Portuguese, German, and Welsh with more languages being offered as series popularity grows. It is the goal of this series to improve global history literacy while inspiring women and men with a more accurate understanding of history. It is the hope of this author and historian that the stage dramas will also help address inequities in the entertainment industry which so far have offered limited opportunities for women, people of colour, and religious minorities.

Thank you for reading this narrative biography. It is my fondest wish you will explore more of the Legendary Women of World History and be inspired!

Share the love of this book and the Legendary Women of World History Series by kindly reviewing this book on your blog, website, and on major retailer websites. Your review not only offers this author your feedback for improvement of this book series, but helps other people find this book so they can enjoy it as well. Only a few sentences and a few minutes of your time is all it takes to share the love with those who want to enjoy it too.

Made in the USA
Las Vegas, NV
25 October 2024

10432618R00069